T&T CLARK STUDY GUIDES TO THE OLD TESTAMENT

Daniel: Sovereignty, Human and Divine

Series Editor
Adrian Curtis, University of Manchester, UK
Published in association with the Society for Old Testament Study

Other titles in the series include:

T&T CLARK STUDY GUIDES TO THE NEW TESTAMENT

Daniel: Sovereignty, Human and Divine

An Introduction and Study Guide

Ernest C. Lucas

t&tclark

LONDON • NEW YORK • OXFORD • NEW DELHI • SYDNEY

T&T CLARK
Bloomsbury Publishing Plc
50 Bedford Square, London, WC1B 3DP, UK
1385 Broadway, New York, NY 10018, USA
29 Earlsfort Terrace, Dublin 2, Ireland

BLOOMSBURY, T&T CLARK and the T&T Clark logo are trademarks of
Bloomsbury Publishing Plc

First published in Great Britain 2023

Cover design by clareturner.co.uk

A catalogue record for this book is available from the British Library

Library of Congress Control Number: 2022037434

ISBN: HB: 978-0-5676-9356-3
PB: 978-0-5676-7683-2
ePDF: 978-0-5676-7684-9
eBook: 978-0-5676-7685-6

Series: T&T Clark Study Guides to the Old Testament

Typeset by Deanta Global Publishing Services, Chennai, India

To find out more about our authors and books visit www.bloomsbury.com and
sign up for our newsletters

Contents

4 Daniel: Resisting pressure 57

5 Daniel: When, who and where? 85

Series preface

How can a potential reader be sure that a Guide to a biblical book is balanced and reliable? One answer is 'If the Guide has been produced under the auspices of an organisation such as the Society for Old Testament Study.'

Founded in 1917, the Society for Old Testament Study (or SOTS as it is commonly known) is a British and Irish society for Old Testament scholars, but with a worldwide membership. It seeks to foster the academic study of the Old Testament/Hebrew Bible in various ways, for example by arranging conferences (usually twice per year) for its members, maintaining links with other learned societies with similar interests in the British Isles and abroad, and producing a range of publications, including scholarly monographs and collections of essays by individual authors or on specific topics. Periodically it has published volumes seeking to provide an overview of recent developments and emphases in the discipline at the time of publication. The annual Society for Old Testament Study Book List, containing succinct reviews by members of the Society of works on the Old Testament and related areas which have been published in the previous year or so, has proved an invaluable bibliographical resource.

With the needs of students in particular in mind, the Society also produced a series of Study Guides to the books of the Old Testament. This first series of Old Testament Guides, published for the Society by Sheffield Academic Press in the 1980s and 1990s, under the general editorship of the late Professor Norman Whybray, was well received as a very useful resource which teachers could recommend to their students with confidence. But it has inevitably become dated with the passage of time, hence the decision that a new series should be commissioned.

The aim of the new series is to continue the tradition established by the first Series, namely to provide a concise, comprehensive, manageable and affordable guide to each biblical book. The intention is that each volume will contain an authoritative overview of the current thinking on the traditional matters of Old Testament/Hebrew Bible introduction, addressing matters of content, major critical issues and theological perspectives, in the light of recent scholarship, and suggesting suitable further reading. Where appropriate to the particular biblical book or books, attention may also be given to less traditional approaches or particular theoretical perspectives.

All the authors are members of the Society, known for their scholarship and with wide experience of teaching in Universities and Colleges. The series general editor, Adrian Curtis, taught Old Testament/Hebrew Bible at the University of Manchester for many years, is a former Secretary of the Society and was President of the Society for 2016.

It is the hope of the Society that these Guides will stimulate in their readers an appreciation of the body of literature whose study is at the heart of all its activities.

Preface

The stories in Daniel 1–6 make it one of the best-known books in the Old Testament, but it is not one of the most frequently studied. The strange, sometimes bizarre, imagery in its dreams and visions and its enigmatic prophecies have made the interpretation of the book controversial among both lay people and scholars. The book also raises several historical problems. Concentration on these issues has often led to neglect of its wider theological message. This study guide tries to do justice to these long-standing debates and controversies. It also, however, seeks to provide an introduction and orientation to fresh approaches to the book which have developed over recent decades. The second half of the twentieth century saw a growing interest in literary approaches to the Old Testament, especially its narratives. This has provided new ways to approach old questions. Intertextuality has become an important aspect of Old Testament study and has considerable relevance to Daniel. Developments in the study of apocalypses and apocalyptic movements also throw helpful light on the book. So do studies of Daniel in the context of ancient Near Eastern literature and history. There has been a rise in 'reader-response' approaches to texts in which readers bring their concerns and perspectives to a text both as a way of uncovering its meaning in its context and of generating interaction between the ancient text and the modern context. In the case of Daniel this has been seen in some political, post-colonial and feminist studies.

Daniel has had a cultural impact out of proportion to its size. Its stories have inspired artists and musicians. Perhaps best known are Rembrandt's painting of Belshazzar's Feast and William Walton's cantata inspired by the same story. Ruben's painting of Daniel in the Lion's Den and William Blake's print of Nebuchadnezzar in his madness are other notable works of art. The book's critique of human rulers has influenced political movements down the centuries. The 'Fifth Monarchy Men' in mid-seventeenth-century England were inspired by the dream in Daniel 2 to agitate for the reform or removal of king and parliament to make way for the coming 'fifth kingdom' – the messianic reign of Christ. The stories of the three young men in the fiery furnace and Daniel in the lion's den have encouraged resistance to oppression. This is evident in *The Martyrs Mirror* (1660) which records accounts of the Anabaptist martyrs of the sixteenth and seventeenth centuries. All this is part of what is now called the 'reception history' of Daniel. This covers a field of literature that is too wide for it to be dealt with in this study guide. A helpful introduction to it is provided by the sections on 'reception history' at the end of each chapter in the commentary on Daniel by C. A. Newsom with B. W. Breed (2014).

This study guide only treats in detail the book of Daniel as found in the Hebrew Bible. A very brief Appendix introduces the 'Additions to Daniel' which are found in the Greek Septuagint and in the Bibles of some Christian churches. Unless otherwise indicated, quotations are taken from the New Revised Standard Version and follow its verse numbering. When it differs, the numbering in the Hebrew Masoretic Text is indicated in square brackets. In contexts in which it might be unclear whether 'Daniel' refers to the book or to its hero, the word is put in italics when it refers to the book. The term 'Judah' is used to refer to the pre-exilic kingdom and 'Judea' is used to refer to the province that became part of various empires following its destruction by Nebuchadnezzar. The inhabitants of both the kingdom and the province, and the exiles from them, are referred to as 'Judeans'.

At the start of Chapters 1–4 of this study guide there are suggested 'investigations' which have been tested in seminars as a way of helping students to begin thinking about the issues discussed in these chapters before reading them. The 'investigation' at the end of Chapter 5 is a prompt to encourage the reader to think through the various views that have been surveyed.

Ernest C. Lucas

Abbreviations

AB	Anchor Bible
ABD	*Anchor Bible Dictionary*
ANET	*Ancient Near Eastern Texts Relating to the Old Testament*
ApOTC	Apollos Old Testament Commentary
BA	*Biblical Archaeologist*
BKAT	Biblischer Kommentar, Altes Testament
CAH	Cambridge Ancient History
CBC	Cambridge Bible Commentary
CBQ	*Catholic Biblical Quarterly*
ConBOT	Coniectanae Biblica: Old Testament Series
DJD	Discoveries in the Judean Desert
EvQ	*Evangelical Quarterly*
FRLANT	Forschungen zur Religion und Literatur des Alten und Neuen Testaments
HDR	Harvard Dissertations in Religion
HO	Handbuch der Orientalistik
HSM	Harvard Semitic Monographs
ICC	International Critical Commentary
JBL	*Journal of Biblical Literature*
JCS	*Journal of Cuneiform Studies*
JSOT	*Journal for the Study of the Old Testament*
JTS	*Journal of Theological Studies*

KTU	*Die keilalphabetischen Texte aus Ugarit*
LXX	Septuagint
MT	Masoretic Text
NIDOTTE	*New International Dictionary of Old Testament Theology and Exegesis*
OTL	Old Testament Library
OTP	*Old Testament Pseudepigepigrapha*
SBLDS	Society of Biblical Literature Dissertation Series
SBT	Studies in Biblical Theology
SBL	Society of Biblical Literature
TAPS	Transactions of the American Philosophical Society
TBC	Torch Bible Commentaries
TCS	Texts from Cuneiform Sources
TGUOS	Transactions of the Glasgow University Oriental Society
TOTC	Tyndale Old Testament Commentary
Vg	Vulgate
VT	*Vetus Testamentum*
VTSup	Supplements to Vetus Testamentum
WBC	Word Biblical Commentary
ZAW	*Zeitschrift für alttestamentlich Wissenschaft*

1

Daniel: The Book

Investigations

1 Read the stories in Dan 1–6 noting the literary form and the contents of each. What do they all have in common? Are there differences which would lead you to separate them into sub-groups?
2 Read the visions in Dan 7–12 and carry out the same exercise as for the stories.
3 After reading the section on the compilation of the book consider what you would propose concerning the possible stages in its compilation.

Introduction

The book of Daniel is somewhat of an enigma. It is a book of two halves since the first six chapters contain stories about Daniel and his friends and the remaining six chapters contain the accounts of visions received by Daniel and reported by him in the first person. The book is written in two languages, Hebrew and Aramaic, but the division does not coincide with that between stories and visions. It begins in Hebrew but at chapter 2:4b changes to Aramaic, which continues until it changes back to Hebrew at the beginning of chapter 8. In the stories, Daniel and his friends, Judean exiles in a foreign royal court, are able to rise to high positions of power despite sometimes facing strong opposition. The visions present a different picture in which this seems an impossibility and in which martyrdom for Judeans who remain faithful to their God is a real possibility. In the Hebrew Bible Daniel is included among 'The Writings' but in the Christian Old Testament the book is one of the 'Major Prophets'. These differences and tensions in the book leave plenty of scope for study and debate about the book's background, formation, purpose and message.

The historical setting

In 612 BCE, Nineveh, the capital of the Neo-Assyrian Empire on the river Tigris, fell to an assault by the combined forces of Babylon, under Nabopolassar, and Media, under Cyaxares. The Assyrian army withdrew to Haran on the river Euphrates but was driven out of there by the Babylonians in 610. When an attack by a joint Assyrian and Egyptian force failed to recapture it, the Neo-Assyrian Empire ceased to exist. For over a century Assyria had been the major super-power in the ancient Near East. The Egyptians tried to prevent the westward spread of Babylonian power but Nebuchadnezzar, the Babylonian crown-prince, defeated them in a battle at Carchemish on the Euphrates in 605 and then crushed them in a battle at Hamath in Syria. Syria, Lebanon and Palestine, including Judah, now came under the control of Babylon. Soon after the battle Nabopolassar died and Nebuchadnezzar became the King of Babylon.

Although Jehoiakim had been put on the throne in Jerusalem as an Egyptian vassal, Nebuchadnezzar left him in place, but he probably took captives and tribute from him as the Babylonian Chronicle (which summarizes the main events in each year of the king's reign) says he did from the kings of Syria-Lebanon. When Nebuchadnezzar failed in an attempt to invade Egypt in 601 Jehoiakim rebelled against him. Nebuchadnezzar was unable to make an immediate response and did not invade Judah until 598. Before he got to Jerusalem Jehoiakim had died and been succeeded by his son Jehoiachin. Nebuchadnezzar captured the city after a siege of three months. He took Jehoiachin, many officials and leading citizens, and much booty off to Babylon, leaving Zedekiah, Jehoiachin's uncle, as his vassal ruler. The Judean leaders were divided into pro-Babylonian and pro-Egyptian factions. In 589 Zedekiah rebelled and Nebuchadnezzar once again besieged Jerusalem. After a siege of eighteen months the walls were breached, the city sacked and the palace and temple burned. Zedekiah fled but was captured, blinded and taken to Babylon in chains. Judah lost all vestiges of independence, becoming a province of the Babylonian Empire with a governor appointed by the Babylonians.

Following Nebuchadnezzar's death in 562 there was a period of instability in Babylon until Nabonidus, who was of a noble family but not the royal line, seized power in 556. He was a worshipper of the Moon God, Sin. This resulted in friction with the priests of Marduk, the patron of the city of Babylon. This may be part of the reason why Nabonidus eventually moved his residence to the oasis of Teima in Arabia and stayed there for ten years. This was also a strategic location for controlling the lucrative Arabian trade routes. He left the crown-prince, Belshazzar, as his Regent in Babylon.

When the Neo-Assyrian Empire fell the Medes took over its northern and eastern provinces, leaving Mesopotamia and the lands to the west to the Babylonians. Under Cyaxares and Astyages the Medes expanded their empire and their power grew to rival or exceed that of Babylon, especially after the death of Nebuchadnezzar. The vassal King of Anshan in southern Persia, Cyrus, rebelled against Astyages and by 550 had captured his capital, Ecbatana, and dethroned him. He campaigned successfully in Asia Minor and to the east. Faced with the threat of Cyrus' growing power Nabonidus returned to Babylon, where the great New Year Festival was held in 539 for the first time since he had moved to Teima. This may have been meant to boost morale and resistance to Cyrus. However, Cyrus had already defeated a Babylonian army at Opis on the Tigris. In 539 his general, named Ugbaru or Gubaru, entered Babylon without a fight. The Babylonian Empire was absorbed into the Persian Empire. A partially broken, barrel-shaped clay cylinder, the 'Cyrus Cylinder', records his policy towards the peoples whom the Babylonians had taken into exile as captives. They were allowed to return to their homelands with the images that had been taken from their sanctuaries. In 538 a large party of exiled Judeans returned to Jerusalem taking with them vessels looted by Nebuchadnezzar from the Jerusalem Temple, with the aim of rebuilding the Temple and re-establishing worship there.

The Persian Empire lasted for just over two centuries. In 336 Alexander the Great came to the throne in Macedonia. In 334 he invaded Asia Minor with the aim of freeing the Greek cities there from Persian control. After defeating the local Persian forces and gaining control of Asia Minor, he defeated the main Persian army under Darius III at the Battle of Issus. He then headed south to Egypt, where he was crowned as Pharaoh in 332. During this campaign Judea came under his control. In 331 he returned to Persia and crushed the Persian army at the Battle of Gaugamela. Darius escaped from the battlefield but was captured and assassinated by one of his satraps. After campaigning in central Asia and north-west India Alexander returned to Babylon, where he died of a fever in 323. Following his death there was a lengthy period of in-fighting among his senior generals. After the Battle of Ipsus in Asia Minor in 301 four 'successor kingdoms' were established. Two of these played a large part in the history of Judea, which lay between them. These were the kingdom of Egypt, established by Ptolemy and that of Seleucus, ruler of Syria and Mesopotamia.

The struggles of their successors over control of the area between them, including Judea, lie behind the visions in *Daniel*. Alexander had introduced a policy of 'Hellenization', of seeking to unite east and west in his empire by introducing Greek culture throughout it. His successors continued this policy. This produced tensions within the Jewish community as they faced this cultural pressure. The Seleucid ruler Antiochus III finally extended his control from Syria to the border of Egypt after the Battle of Paneas in 198 BCE. He treated the Jews favourably. After his death in 187 he was succeeded by his elder son Seleucus IV and, after his murder in 175, by his younger son Antiochus IV, who adopted a very different attitude towards the Jews. He supported pro-Hellenists in Jerusalem and with their connivance, plundered the temple there in 169. Eventually, apparently exasperated by the religious intransigence of the orthodox Jews, he instigated severe persecution of them in 167, outlawing traditional Jewish religious practices on pain of death and desecrating the temple. It was rededicated to the god Zeus/Jupiter, whose image was set up in it, and swine flesh was offered on the altar of burnt offerings. This provoked an armed revolt, of which Judas Maccabeus eventually became the leader. He carried out a successful campaign against Antiochus' forces in Judea and took over the whole of Jerusalem, apart from the Acra. This was a colony of Hellenized Gentiles and renegade Jews. Judas and his followers purified and rededicated the temple in December 164, instituting the annual Feast of Hannukah ('Dedication'). At about this time Antiochus IV met an untimely death while trying to rob a temple in Persia.

The stories

Stories consist of several different elements. Every story has a *setting*. This may be purely internal, relating to the world of the story, or it may relate to the world outside the story. All the stories in Dan 1–6 are set in the courts of various ancient Near Eastern kings. This makes them stories about Judean exiles but also serves to place the stories within the time-line of Judah's history as it is presented in the Hebrew Bible.

A story has a *plot*. The Greek philosopher Aristotle said that a good plot has a beginning, a middle and an end. Some kind of problem arises at the beginning of the story. As the narrative progresses through its middle various complications arise, and the problem is finally resolved at the end. It does not take much thought about the stories in Daniel to realize that in them there are two basic kinds of plot. In Dan 3 and 6 the problem is that the envy of certain royal officials puts Daniel or his companions in life-threatening situations, from which they are delivered in a miraculous way. In the other stories Daniel is faced with a difficult problem which the rest of the king's officials cannot solve. With God's help he succeeds in solving the problem and receives a reward. These two different kinds of plot might be called 'conflict stories' and 'contest stories'. Although Dan 1 contains a contest story it is more complicated than the others. King Nebuchadnezzar's decree about the training of the Judean exiles as sages creates, unbeknown to the king, a problem for Daniel and his companions. When Daniel takes the problem to the palace official who is in charge of their training, the official cannot see any solution to it. Daniel then suggests a solution, which sets up an implicit contest between him and his companions and the other trainee sages. Thanks to God's blessing, Daniel and his friends win the contest and receive the king's accolade. This story is more complicated because it is not a free-standing contest story but also acts as an introduction to the book as whole. This is the main function of vv. 1–7 but they also lead into the contest story in the following verses.

The actions which make up the plot of a story are generated by the story's *characters*. There are various ways of classifying characters. Three main kinds of characters appear in the stories in Daniel. There are 'rounded' characters who show a variety of character traits. Others are 'type' characters who typify one main trait. 'Agent' characters simply fulfil a function in the plot. For example, in Dan 6 both King Darius and Daniel are rounded characters, each showing a range of actions and emotions. The 'chief ministers and satraps' typify the envious courtier. The angel who shuts the mouth of the lions is simply an agent. Because they contain a high proportion of types and agents the stories in Dan 1–6 have a cartoon-like nature because of the use of stereotypes and simplification of the story.

Authors can use various methods of *characterization*. In general, Hebrew narratives use little in the way of detailed description to create characters. For this reason, when it does occur, as in the description of the Judean exiles in Dan 1:3–4, it is probably significant for the plot or the meaning of the story. The main method of characterization in Hebrew narrative is through the words and actions of the character, or what others say about him or her. Belshazzar's actions in Dan 5:2 show his disdain for the God of the Judeans. It is striking how Daniel's character is built up through the stories by what others think and say about him. It begins with Nebuchadnezzar's assessment of the abilities of Daniel and his companions in Dan 1:18–20 and continues with his prostration before, and promotion of, Daniel (2:46–48) and recognition of Daniel as one 'endowed with the spirit of the holy gods' (4:8–9), an accolade that is repeated by the Queen in Dan 5:11. Finally, there is the testimony of those who are seeking his downfall in Dan 6:4–5, who 'could find no complaint or corruption against him' and no grounds for charges against him unless it was 'in connection with the law of his God'.

A story can be told from a number of viewpoints, which might be that of the narrator or one of the characters. Various techniques can be used to change the viewpoint within a story. Daniel 4 is unusual in the number of changes that take place. It begins with Nebuchadnezzar's viewpoint, expressed in the first person in a letter (vv. 1–18). In vv. 19–27 it changes to Daniel's viewpoint as he addresses the king. The narrator takes over in vv. 28–33, giving an account of what happened to Nebuchadnezzar. The story concludes by returning to Nebuchadnezzar's first-person account of what happened.

A number of different genre classifications have been suggested for the stories in *Daniel*, such as novel, romance, legend and wisdom tale (Collins, 1993: 42). However, stories specifically about courtiers seem to have been quite popular in the ancient Near East and to form a distinct type of story. Two others are found in the Hebrew Bible. The story of the Jew Mordecai and his opponent Haman is a sub-plot in the Book of Esther which, like Dan 6, is set in the Persian court. It is a conflict story. There is also the story of Joseph and Pharaoh's dream in Gen 41, which is a contest story. Several stories about courtiers are known from ancient Egypt (Redford, 1970: 87–105). The best known are those about Sinuhe and Wenamun. The only story about a courtier known from Mesopotamia is that about Ahikar. Although it originated in Assyria it was known to the Jews since an Aramaic version of it was found at

Elephantine in southern Egypt, where there was a Jewish colony. The Greek writer Herodotus recounts a number of stories about courtiers (Wills, 1990: 55–70).

The similarities between the stories in this corpus of 'court tales' suggest that they had at least three purposes. First, they were written to entertain those who heard or read them. For most of them the royal court was probably a rather exotic location and renowned courtiers were celebrities. The stories would have the same kind of attraction and interest as those about modern celebrities do for many today. One aspect of entertainment is humour. As noted already, the occurrence of 'type' characters in the stories gives them something of a cartoon nature, which supplies an element of humour. There are other forms of humour too. It is hard to read the first half of Dan 3, especially aloud, with a straight face because of the frequently repeated long lists of officials, peoples and musical instruments. Then there is also the robot-like reaction of the people as they all fall down as soon as the musicians strike up. There is humorous irony in Dan 6 as Darius is tricked into passing a law to prove his power only to find that he is trapped by his own law, powerless to save Daniel from its consequences. The fact that the stories were written to entertain does not mean that they are necessarily completely fictional. Some of them may be about real people (e.g. there is evidence that someone called Ahikar held high office under Esarhaddon, VanderKam, 1992) and be rooted in actual events. However, they are the result of the art of the storyteller rather than the concerns of a scholarly historian. They lie somewhere on the continuum that runs from imaginative writing to historical reporting. It is often not possible for us to say where a particular story lies on this continuum.

Secondly, many of the 'court tales' seem to have been intended to educate and edify their hearers and readers as well as entertain them. Stories have always been a good means to this end. Imaginative storytelling draws the readers or hearers into the story so that they identify with the characters, sharing their values and motivations as they face problems, and hopefully learning from this. An excessive concern about the historicity of a story can get in the way of appreciating its educational purpose. Truth and fiction are not mutually exclusive because there are different kinds of truth. A well-researched historical-novel may give a truer account of what it was like to take part in an event and the lessons that can be learnt from it than can be given in a scholarly historical monograph about the event. However, if the story is to persuade people to accept and live by the moral, theological or other claims it is making the hearers and readers need to be able to make some connection between the story and events in the real world outside the story in which they live.

Finally, some of the 'court tales' are about courtiers in the service of a foreign king. These seem to have the added purpose of encouraging conquered peoples to maintain their sense of ethnic identity and worth, while also taking a positive attitude towards their situation. Sometimes this may be an attempt to bolster belief in some kind of inherent ethnic superiority. In the stories in Daniel, the source of identity and worth is trust in the Most High God, who rules supreme over human rulers and their affairs. This trust is modelled by the faithfulness to their God shown by Daniel and his companions (Wills, 1990). In fact, the court setting of the stories serves to highlight that the underlying issue is that of sovereignty, both divine and human, and the claims they make on people. They are theological stories while also being entertaining.

The visions in Daniel 7 and 8

The second half of Daniel contains reports of four visionary experiences. Daniel's experience of the first of these is described as both a 'dream' and a 'vision' (7:1–2). In a study of dream reports from the ancient Near East, Oppenheim (1956: 187) found that they had a 'surprisingly uniform' pattern. The reports in Dan 7 and 8 fit into this pattern.

Introduction	7:1	8:1
Report of the vision	7:2–27	8:2–25
The end of the vision	7:28a	8:26
Daniel's reaction	7:28b	8:27

The reports Oppenheim studied sometimes also included, at the end, the actual fulfilment of what was predicted or promised in the dream.

Dreams were an important form of divination in the ancient Near East. Collections of 'dream omens' were compiled and diviners would consult these when seeking to interpret the meaning of a dream. In the Hebrew Bible dreams are recognized as an authentic means of revelation from God. It is sometimes argued that Deut 13:1–5 [MT 2–6] and Jer 23:25–32 are evidence that dreams came to be viewed with distrust in the later pre-exilic period. In both these passages, however, the issue at stake is not a distrust of dreams in themselves as a means of divine communication. In both passages the false prophets are not identified by the means by which they get their message (in Jer 23:16 these same prophets receive visions) but the content of the message itself. What is notable in the Hebrew tradition is that the interpretation of dreams or visions is not a divinatory skill requiring the use of omen collections. Instead, the dreams are self-interpreting (as God or an angel speaks directly to the dreamer in the dream) or the interpreter receives the interpretation as a result of special God-given wisdom (as in the stories of Joseph and Daniel).

The visions in Dan 7 and 8 are *symbolic visions*, because what is seen in them are images and actions that symbolize something else. Niditch (1983), among others, has argued for a development in the form of symbolic visions in the tradition of the Hebrew prophets. She identified three major stages in the development. The first stage is to be found in the visions of pre-exilic prophets, in particular the visions in Amos 7–8 and Jer 1 and 24. These open with an indication of a visionary experience followed by a description of the vision (or this may come later). God then asks the prophet what he has seen and the prophet replies by giving or repeating the description of the vision. The interpretation is then given by God. The language used is simple and rhythmic with short sentences. The repetition of key terms binds the account into a unity. The symbol is quite simple (a plumb-line, a basket of figs) and its interpretation fairly straightforward, sometimes using word-play.

The second stage appears in the early post-exilic period, especially in the visions of Zech 1–6. These vary somewhat in form but the main change that occurs in all of them is that God is replaced by an angel as the interpreter, and there is no use of word-play. Sometimes the prophet takes the initiative in asking for the interpretation. The symbols that appear in the visions are more complex, as is their relationship to the meaning. The account of the vision is longer, becoming a prose narrative. In a few cases the account ends with a charge to the prophet.

The visions in Dan 7–8 represent the third stage. The main new feature is the reporting of the reactions of the prophet. A sense of fear motivates the request for the interpretation and then an account of his reactions forms the conclusion of the account. The imagery used has become much more complex, even somewhat bizarre. Collins (1993: 54–5) has compared these visions to visions in what he calls 'historical apocalypses' of the late centuries

BCE and early centuries CE (these will be discussed in the next chapter). He finds a shared form.

Circumstances of the vision	7:1	8:1
Description of the vision	7:2–14	8:2–14
Request for an interpretation	7:15–16	8:15–18
Interpretation by an angel	7:17–18	8:19–26a
Second request	7:19–22	
Second interpretation	7:23–27	
Charge to the prophet		8:26b
The prophet's reaction	7:28	8:27

This follows the same general pattern as the dream report but with the main section of the report analysed in more detail. The appearance of the interpreting angel in the second and third stages seems to be a way of emphasizing the transcendence of God. The increasing complexity of the symbols used increases the sense of awe and mystery associated with the revelation, which is emphasized further by the prophet's reactions to it in the third stage.

The symbols used in Daniel's visions should not be regarded as mere ciphers in a random code that needs to be 'cracked'. These symbols draw on images, ideas and stereotypes of a culture shared by the visionary and those to whom the visions were originally reported. As a result, they carried associated sentiments and values. This gave them a 'feel' and impact that simple ciphers do not have. Modern readers of Daniel do not share that culture. The search to capture something of the cultural meaning and significance of the symbols has led to extensive discussion and debate about the religio-historical background of the imagery, which will be discussed in Chapter 3.

The visions in Daniel 9–12

The vision reports in Dan 9–12 do not follow the pattern of those in Dan 7–8. They also differ in another way. These are not *symbolic visions* but *epiphany visions* because in them what the prophet sees is a supernatural figure who conveys a verbal revelation, not a vision containing symbolic imagery. Although there are differences in the balance of the elements in these visions, they do share the same overall structure.

Circumstances	9:1–2	10:1
Supplication	9:3–11	10:2–3
Appearance of messenger	9:20–21	10:4–9
Word of assurance	9:22–23	10:10–11:1
Revelation	9:24–27	11:2–12:3
Charge to prophet		12:4

The 'supplication' in Dan 9 is a lengthy prayer prompted by what Daniel has read in Jeremiah's prophecies about the length of the period of exile in Babylon. Having begun with the confession of Israel's sin it moves into supplication. It has close parallels with other post-exilic prayers: Ezra 9:6–15; Neh 1:5–11; 9:5–37; Ps 79. Theologically there are parallels in both thought and language with Lev 26:27–45 (Fishbane, 1988: 487). The identification of the supernatural messenger as Gabriel provides a link back to Dan 8:16. In Dan 10–12 the 'supplication' takes the form of a three-week fast (10:2) but it becomes clear that the aim of this was to 'gain understanding', presumably about the previous revelation, and had included verbal prayer (10:12). The length of the revelation is much greater in Dan 10–12 and it ends with a formal charge to the prophet, which is lacking in Dan 9.

There is no near parallel to the form of these visions elsewhere in the Hebrew Bible. Also, the content and style of the revelation is new in the Hebrew tradition: a quite detailed survey of future history which is presented in short, enigmatic sentences. Daniel 8:23–25 does share these characteristics. The use of the phrase 'the beautiful land' (8:9; 11:16, 41) and the motif of the king who assaults heaven also links chs 8 and 11. In the other prophetic books of the Hebrew Bible the predictive prophecies relate to a single event or situation. The only extended historical surveys in the Hebrew prophets are in Ezek 16; 20; 23. These, however, are concerned mainly with the past and are a way of exposing the sin of Israel and Judah and their readiness for judgement, although they do end with a statement of what God will do in the near future. They present history in broad outline only and their style is different: Ezek 16 is in ordinary prose and Ezek 16 and 23 are allegories whose meaning is clear, especially in the light of the established use in the prophets of the marriage relationship as a picture of the covenant relationship of God to Israel. The lack of parallels to the content and style of these revelations in the Hebrew tradition suggests the need to look elsewhere. As we shall see, there are some parallels in the 'historical apocalypses' and in a group of Akkadian texts.

The languages of Daniel

The Hebrew Bible consists of a sufficiently large corpus of Hebrew documents whose origins are spread over several centuries for it to be possible to recognize changes in the language over time. The Hebrew of Daniel has more in common with the Late Biblical Hebrew of Ezra, Nehemiah and Chronicles than it does with the Hebrew of Ezekiel, which reflects the language of the exilic period. A full, detailed, comparison of the Hebrew of Daniel and that of Hebrew documents from Qumran has yet to be made. However, there are some clear differences between them: for example, the Qumran documents make much more use of a few consonants to represent long vowels (so-called 'vowel letters') and of first-person exhortation verb forms in the place of the normal form (pseudo-cohortatives) than is found in Daniel. Collins (1993: 20–2) places the Hebrew of Daniel somewhere between that of Chronicles and the Qumran documents.

It is now generally accepted that the Aramaic used in Daniel is the Official Aramaic which was in use from about 700 to 200 BCE. The Aramaic documents from Qumran use the later Middle Aramaic of 200 BCE to 200 CE. After a survey of comparisons of the Aramaic of Daniel with that used in the material from Elephantine (fifth century), Samaria (fourth century) and Qumran (second century and later), Collins (1993: 15–17) concludes that the Aramaic of Daniel is later than that of the Samaria papyri but earlier than that of the Dead Sea Scrolls. A weakness of this approach is the widespread geographical area from which the material comes and the implicit assumption that linguistic developments would have occurred more or less uniformly throughout the area.

Attempts have been made to date the language of Daniel on the basis of the presence of Persian and Greek loan-words. There are about twenty recognized Persian loan-words, nearly all in the Aramaic portion. The debate has been about whether or not these are all Old Persian words. Collins questions this (1993:18–19) but accepts that the presence of these words is compatible with a late sixth-century date but prefers a rather later date to allow for extensive linguistic borrowing. There are only three indisputable Greek loan-words. All are found in the lists in Dan 3:5, 7, 15: *kitharis* (קַתְרוֹס, lyre), *psaltērion* (פְּסַנְתֵּרִין, harp) and *symphonia* (סוּמְפֹּנְיָה, musical ensemble). Coxon (1973) argues that Greek contact with the ancient Near East is attested from the eighth century onwards and that in a specialized area, like music, Greek influence might have been significant quite early on. He concludes that the presence of these loan-words in Daniel is 'neutral' with regard to dating the Aramaic.

The compilation of the book

Since at least the time of the Jewish philosopher Benedict Spinoza in the late seventeenth century and the physicist Sir Isaac Newton, who was fascinated by Daniel's visions, in the early eighteenth century, there have been attempts to explain the enigma of Daniel by theories about how the book was compiled. They have involved postulating several stages in the growth of the book and usually several authors. These theories have multiplied in the last two hundred years. None has found widespread acceptance. This is not surprising considering the number of different features of the book that need to be taken into account. Having discussed most of these above, we can bring them together and consider what they might contribute to understanding the process of compilation of the book

The first half of the book contains stories, told in the third person, about Judeans who are living in exile as courtiers in the court of a foreign king. They fit into a fairly popular genre of literature in the ancient Near East, the 'court tale'. All, but the first story, are written in a form of Official Aramaic, the kind of language that one might expect to be used for a popular story since it was the language commonly used for communication throughout the region. Although there are questions about the historicity of a few specific points in the stories, it is generally accepted that they give an authentic picture of life in the royal court of the late Babylonian and early Persian period. The rulers are depicted as being willing to employ faithful Judeans in their service, and to promote them according to their ability. They are generally prepared to tolerate their religion, though at times this tolerance runs out, especially when other courtiers, envious of the Judeans, find reasons to turn the king against them. They can then find that their lives are in danger. Comparison of these stories with other tales about courtiers in foreign courts suggests that an important purpose of these stories is to commend a lifestyle for Judeans in the eastern diaspora (Humphreys, 1973). Somewhat in the spirit of Jeremiah's letter to the exiles, 'seek the peace and prosperity of the city to which I [the LORD] have carried you into exile. Pray to the LORD for it, because if it prospers, you too will prosper' (Jer 29:7, New International Version), the stories encourage the Judeans to get involved in the society in which they find themselves. They suggest that they can prosper there, provided they remain faithful to their God, though there is also recognition that their faithfulness will be put to the test and they will sometimes face oppression, even serious persecution. The change of language remains a puzzle. It happens at an appropriate point, when the Babylonian courtiers first address King Nebuchadnezzar. However, if the stories were written for a popular readership, why put the first one in Hebrew, a language with which many of them would struggle? It is clearly an important introduction to the following stories. It provides the setting that lies behind all of them. The Judean characters in the stories are introduced with both their Hebrew and Babylonian names, which are picked up in the later stories. The report of the bringing of articles from the temple in Jerusalem to Babylon (1:2) prepares the ground for the story in Dan 5.

The second half of the book contains first-person reports of four visions. The first two fit into the general pattern for dream reports in the ancient Near East but also into a developing tradition of symbolic visions in the Hebrew prophets. The third and fourth visions are epiphany visions which have no close parallels elsewhere in the Hebrew Bible. The first vision is written in Aramaic but the rest are written in a form of Late Biblical Hebrew, just how 'late' is open to some debate. Despite the change in language, the opening of the second vision (8:1) clearly links it to the first. The third vision contains a clear allusion back to the second one (9:21), thereby linking the epiphany visions to the symbolic visions. The fourth vision is linked to the second by its form and the phrase 'the beautiful land'. In the visions, world rulers are depicted as arrogant and ungodly, even sometimes being openly opposed to God. Some of them oppress the 'people of the holy ones of the Most High', making war against them and killing some. Most modern scholars conclude that the background here is the persecution of the Jews by the ruler of the Seleucid Empire, Antiochus IV Epiphanes, in the first half of the second century BCE. Because the visions show a concern about Jerusalem and the temple it is generally assumed that the visions originated in Judea. However, this is not necessarily so. Jews in the diaspora could have a passionate concern about them too, as shown in Ps 137 and Neh 1. It is often suggested that the use of Hebrew in reporting the visions was thought appropriate because it gives them an aura of mystery and makes them seem more esoteric. It is argued that this fits with the charge of secrecy given to

Daniel (12:4). This, of course, highlights the problem that the first vision is recorded in Aramaic.

Not only is there the problem that the division of the languages does not match the division of the literary genres. There is a less obvious puzzling feature, though one that most commentators have noted. This is that chs 2–7 form a chiastic group that seems unlikely to be a result of chance.

A1 A dream about four earthly kingdoms and God's kingdom (ch. 2)
B1 A story about Jews being faithful in the face of death (ch. 3)
C1 A story about royal hubris, which is humbled (ch. 4)
C2 A story about royal hubris which, is humbled (ch. 5)
B2 A story about a Jew who is faithful in the face of death (ch. 6)
A2 A vision about four earthly kingdoms and God's kingdom (ch. 7)

A striking feature in this grouping is that the series of stories in chs 1–6 has its own coherent time-line and so does the sequence of visions in chs 7–12. However, the vision in ch. 7 is set before the event in ch. 5, an indication that it was added to the stories after they had been put into a coherent collection.

It was the combination of stories written in the third person about Daniel and reports of visions in the first person by Daniel that led Spinoza and Newton to realize that the book as we know it must have had a compiler who brought the two collections together. They both assumed that the accounts of the visions were written by Daniel himself in the early Persian period, a view that a minority of scholars would defend today. This raises the question of whether the compiler was the author of the stories about Daniel. Because of differences which he saw between some of the stories Newton thought that they were probably originally independent pieces which the compiler brought together. Many modern scholars take a similar view. In arguing for the stories having independent origins, they point to various features in them. It is argued that it is hard to reconcile the date in Dan 2:1 with the statement in Dan 1:5, 18 that Daniel and his friends had three years of training before entering the king's service. There is also Nebuchadnezzar's apparent lack of knowledge of someone he had recognized as an outstanding student. Some see the absence of any hint of Daniel in the story in Dan 3 as odd. Daniel 4 has a very different form from the other stories, being largely a letter written in the first person by Nebuchadnezzar. Belshazzar's father was Nabonidus, not Nebuchadnezzar as stated in Dan. 5. This is taken as indicating that a story which originally named Nabonidus has been altered to make the reference back to Dan 1:1–2 stronger. In the Greek translation of the Hebrew Bible, the Septuagint, there is a story about Daniel titled *Bel and the Dragon* (or *Serpent*). It includes an episode in which Daniel is thrown into a lions' den, as in Dan 6. The two stories are very different. Although Daniel is a companion of King Cyrus in *Bel and the Dragon* the story is not a court tale. It is a polemic against idolatry. In this story Daniel's opponents are not courtiers but priests and it is Daniel who takes the initiative in producing conflict. There are no grounds for supposing any interdependence between *Bel and the Dragon* and Dan 6 but the sharing of the common element about the lions' den has been taken as evidence that behind both lies an older story about Daniel which included it, and of a developing tradition of independent stories about Daniel. The validity and significance of these points is a matter of debate, but they do make the question of the origin and authorship of the stories in Daniel an open question.

Whether or not the compiler was author of the stories, in their current form they make a unified corpus. The later stories allude to, or assume information from, the first story. There is a unified theme and theology running through them. The first story plays a key role in this. Its opening (1:1–2) and closing (1:21) historical notices set the time-line for the stories. The Judean characters are introduced and the reason for their role in the court is explained (1:3–7, 18–20). The story of court contest (1:8–17) sets the theme for the following stories. Two questions about Dan 1 have been the subject of debate. The first is whether or not a simpler story of court contest lies behind it, which has been developed to provide the introductory story. No one has produced a reconstruction of this possible story which has found general acceptance, so this remains a conjecture. The second is whether or not Dan 1:1–2:4a was originally composed in Aramaic, like the other stories, so that they all once circulated as a collection of Aramaic stories about Daniel and his companions. It is then postulated that the opening story was translated into Hebrew when the stories were combined with the collection of visions as a way of binding the two collections together, with a suitable transition point being chosen for the shift to Aramaic. As evidence that it might be a translation from Aramaic it is pointed out that it contains a higher density of Aramaisms than the Hebrew in Dan 7–12 and that it contains two of the three Persian loan-words that occur in the Hebrew in Daniel (פַּרְתְּמִים, *partəmîm*, nobility, 1:3; פַּתְבַּג, *patbag*, royal rations, 1:8). It is also argued that it can be readily back-translated into Aramaic (Koch, 1986). None of this is strong evidence of translation from Aramaic but it is compatible with that possibility.

We have seen that the vision accounts are linked to one another by some literary markers. They also share a common theological outlook. There is also a progression in their focus. The vision in Dan 7 covers four earthly empires but the vision in Dan 8 brings the focus down to two and there is mention of the desecration of the temple in Jerusalem. In Dan. 9:24–27 the focus becomes the impact of the last two empires on Judah and the temple. This is dealt with in much more detail in Dan 11. The fact that the first vision account is in Aramaic cuts across this sense of unity. The Hebrew of chs 8–12 has been described as 'idiosyncratic' or 'awkward' and it contains some Aramaisms. A few scholars have suggested that these chapters were originally composed in Aramaic. However, the arguments they have put forward have not been found convincing. It has been pointed out that many of the features claimed to be evidence of 'translation Hebrew' are found in Second Temple Hebrew. The Aramaisms and awkwardness of the Hebrew could be the result of the author being bilingual but more at home in Aramaic than Hebrew. The dreams in chs 2 and 7 share the motif of a sequence of four earthly empires. However, there are considerable differences between them. Nebuchadnezzar's dream is presented within the narrative of a court tale whereas ch. 7 is simply a self-standing dream report. The imagery differs greatly and in ch. 7 both it and the interpretation are much more complex. As is the case with the court tales and visions in general, the social and historical setting is different, with the visions depicting the earthly rulers and the prospect for the Judeans in a much more negative way. This makes it unlikely that, as a few have suggested, Dan 7 was composed in Aramaic to go with Dan 2–6 and that these six chapters once circulated as a single book which was later combined with the other visions and with the story in Dan 1 added at that time.

Proponents of a post-colonial reading of Daniel have suggested an explanation of the two languages in the book in the light of it being a form of resistance literature. They argue that it begins in Hebrew to evoke the special history and traditions of Judah as God's covenant people. The change to Aramaic, the *lingua franca* of the ancient Near Eastern empires, marks the change brought about by the Babylonian exile. This resulted in the need to cope with the competing claims on identity and allegiance to God and/or the emperor. In the view of the compiler(s) of Daniel the edict of Antiochus IV proscribing practice of the Jewish religion made any accommodation with the emperor impossible. The vision in Dan 7 marks this decisive shift. In the language of the empire, it refutes its claims and predicts its end. The return to Hebrew in Dan 8–12 presents visions which call for rejection of any allegiance to the emperor and adherence to the covenant relationship with God (Portier-Young, 2011, 228).

If, as most modern scholars think, the vision accounts were written and circulated as a collection in the time of Antiochus IV (175–164 BCE), who persecuted the Jews, there is not much time for there to be several stages of development leading to the book as we know it because this seems to be the form of the book that was known at Qumran by the late second century BCE. This allows for a period of no more than about fifty years, and the production and circulation of different editions of the book would have involved the relatively slow process of writing and copying it by hand. The earliest fragment of Daniel from Qumran, 4QDan^c, contains portions of Dan 10 in Hebrew and is dated to the late second century BCE. 4QDan^a attests the change from Aramaic to Hebrew at the end of ch. 7 and beginning of ch. 8, and is dated to the mid-first century BCE. The change from Hebrew to Aramaic in ch. 2:4 is attested in 1QDan^b, which is dated to the first century CE. (For a good, brief, summary of the Qumran texts relevant to *Daniel*, see Newsom, 2014: 3–4.)

So, despite two centuries or more of discussion and debate no consensus has been reached about the compilation of the Book of Daniel and the enigma it presents has not been resolved.

Daniel: Prophecy and apocalyptic

Investigations

1 In Chapter 1 we noted Niditch's study of the development of symbolic visions in the Hebrew prophets. Read Amos 7:7–9 and Jer 24:1–10 and analyse them according to her outline of pre-exilic reports of symbolic visions:

Indication of a vision
Description of the vision
God's question to the prophet
The prophet's reply
The interpretation given by God

Do the same for the vision in Zech 6:1–8 using the outline she gives for a post-exilic report of a symbolic vision:

Indication of a vision
Description of the vision
Question by the prophet
Answer given by an angel
Observation of divine activity
Word spoken to the prophet by the angel

2 Read the oracle about the destruction of Babylon in Isa 13 and the destruction of 'Babylon' (i.e. Rome) in Rev 17 and 18. What are the similarities and differences?

Daniel and Hebrew prophecy

In the Christian Old Testament Daniel is placed among the prophetic books. In the Hebrew Bible, however, it is in the section called 'The Writings' and not in that called 'The Prophets'. The reason for this is unclear. Some think that it is a result of the late date of the origin of the book. However, we do not know when 'The Prophets' came to be regarded as a distinct collection of authoritative Hebrew Scriptures. The earliest reference to it is in the Prologue to the book known as the *Wisdom of Jesus ben Sirach* or *Ecclesiasticus*. This Prologue was written in 132 BCE and in it the writer refers three times to 'the Law, the Prophets, and the other books'. Others suggest that the placing of Daniel in 'The Writings' reflects a recognition that the book is a different kind of literature than the books of the prophets found in 'The Prophets' and that the reports of dreams and visions in the book differ from the oracles and visions recorded in these other books.

An obvious difference about Daniel is its structure: a collection of narratives combined with a collection of vision reports. Some of the prophetic books do contain narratives about the prophet whose oracles they contain but these are more like biographical anecdotes about the actions and experiences of the prophet. They are not crafted, as the stories in Daniel seem to be, with the threefold purpose of entertainment, education and encouragement to remain firm in one's commitment to God.

The Hebrew prophets are often said to be the champions or spokespersons of the special covenant relationship between Israel and Judah and their God, YHWH. In general, the pre-exilic prophets challenge the nation, and especially its leaders, by exposing ways in which they are ignoring or deliberately breaking the covenant and so being unfaithful to YHWH. There were both blessings and curses associated with the covenant (Lev 26; Deut 28) and the pre-exilic prophets warned their hearers that they were in danger of facing, or are even beginning to experience, the covenant curses because of their behaviour. They call on the people to repent and amend their ways before it is too late. Once Jerusalem and the Davidic Kingdom have fallen, and the temple been destroyed, the exilic prophets begin to bring promises of hope, of restoration and renewal. The post-exilic prophets Haggai and Zechariah encourage the returned exiles to get on with the work of rebuilding the temple and re-establishing the worship of YHWH there. Where does Daniel fit into this tradition of prophecy?

In the stories, the only people to whom Daniel has a prophetic ministry are Gentile kings. He urges them to recognize and accept the sovereignty of the Most High God. However, the stories themselves have the purpose of encouraging the Judean exiles to remain faithful to their God. The vision reports are not addressed specifically to any particular audience, though we shall see that their message is intended to encourage Judeans facing persecution to stand firm in their commitment to YHWH. The one place where Daniel appears clearly as a champion of the covenant between YHWH and Israel is in his prayer in Dan 9.

Scholars differ over the origin of this prayer. Some (e.g. Hartman and Di Lella, 1978: 245–6) argue that it is a secondary addition. The following are the main arguments for this.

1 The prayer is written in free-flowing Hebrew, full of traditional phrases and free of Aramaisms. This is markedly different from the rest of the Hebrew in Dan. 8–12.

2 It is a communal confession of sin, whereas the context requires a prayer for illumination.

3 The beginning (vv. 3–4a) and end of the prayer (vv. 20–21a) contain duplications that can be explained as the kind of thing that may happen when a pre-existing section is inserted into a text. There is a smooth transition from v. 3 to v. 21.

4 In both language and thought the prayer has features not found elsewhere in Daniel, for example the use of the divine name YHWH, emphasis on the sin of Israel and on the punitive nature of her suffering.

Others (e.g. Goldingay, 2019: 456–8) find these arguments inconclusive and argue that the prayer was composed by the author of the chapter. They argue that the character of the Hebrew is to be explained by the author using traditional liturgical phraseology. They point to close parallels in the post-exilic prayers of confession in Ezra 9 and Neh 1; 9. In their view the context does not require a prayer of illumination. Daniel's reaction to the prophecy in Jeremiah, as marked by his actions in v. 3, is not one of bewilderment at the meaning of the seventy years but one of distress at the continuing desolation of Jerusalem. The communal confession of sin is just what is recommended in Lev 26:40 as a means of bringing the exile in a foreign land to an end. Fishbane (1988: 489) suggests that the use of forms of the Hebrew root *šmm* ('lay waste, desolate') and the term 'their sin/iniquity' (*'ōnām*) in Jer 25:12 and Lev 26:32–35, 40 explains the connection between the two passages. The repetition at the beginning and end of the prayer, it is argued, is no greater than elsewhere in Daniel's prose, including 9:1–2a. Although there are features of the prayer that are not found elsewhere in Daniel, they are congruent with the theology of the book. The stories, and even more so the visions, assume a special relationship between God and Israel. The visions demonstrate a concern about the desolation of Jerusalem. That there are some in Judah who 'forsake the holy covenant' is made clear in Dan. 11:30.

Some scholars (e.g. Newsom, 2014: 288–9) conclude that although the prayer was probably not written by the author of ch. 9, it was an existing prayer which the author purposefully chose for this context. He drew on its vocabulary in the narrative section. Fishbane (1988: 487–9), however, argues that the evidence of a careful integration of the prayer into its context is such that it indicates common authorship. For example, there is the use of the Hebrew root *šmm* ('desolate, desolation') in vv. 17–18 and vv. 26–27; the use of the root *ntk* ('poured out') in v. 11 and v. 27; the use of the root *śkl* in v. 2 ('perceived'), v. 13 ('reflecting on') and v. 22 ('understanding').

The balance of the argument seems to be in favour of the prayer, whatever its origin, being an original part of the vision account in Dan 9. This locates Daniel in the tradition of the Hebrew prophets.

Another difference between Daniel and the books in 'The Prophets' in the Hebrew Bible is that whereas they are predominantly collections of what were originally spoken oracles, Daniel contains only dreams and visions with their interpretations. We saw in Chapter 1 that Niditch traces a line of development in the form and content of the vision accounts from those in the early classical Hebrew prophets to those in Daniel. But why is there a shift to the exclusive use of dreams and visions? It has been suggested that the increasing prominence of visions in Ezekiel, Zechariah and Daniel is the result of Babylonian influence on exilic and post-exilic Hebrew prophecy. Oracular prophecy did exist in Mesopotamia (Nissinen, 2000). Collections of prophetic oracles have survived in the royal archives of Mari (eighteenth century BCE) and Neo-Assyria (seventh century BCE) but this seems to have been much less important in Mesopotamian culture than the use of various forms of omen divination, including dream omens. There may be some validity in this suggestion, but it has also been argued that the increase in visions and other 'ecstatic' experiences in Ezekiel is the resurfacing of an aspect of Hebrew prophecy which goes back to before the earlier canonical prophets (Carley, 1975). There are a number of references to 'the hand of YHWH' being upon Ezekiel to indicate some kind of ecstatic state (Ezek 1:3; 3:14, 22; 8:1; 33:22; 37:1; 40:1). The only strict parallels to this in the Hebrew Bible are with reference to Elijah (1 Kgs 18:46) and Elisha (2 Kgs 3:15). There are also references to the Spirit lifting Ezekiel up and taking him to another place in a visionary experience (Ezek 3:12, 14; 8:3; 11:1, 24; 43:5). According to 2 Kgs 2:16 Elijah's disciples believed that the Spirit could transfer him from one place to another. Even earlier than this, in stories related to Samuel, ecstatic experience with associated abnormal behaviour is referred to as something expected of prophets (1 Sam 10:9–13; 19:20–24). How far this is relevant to Daniel is questionable. When he falls into an ecstatic state it is in response to a vision and when a heavenly being touches him it is to give him strength. However, it is good to be reminded that the picture we get of Hebrew prophets and prophecy in the canonical books is only a partial one and that there is a wider and more varied context of prophetic experience and behaviour in Israel and Judah.

The interest that the author of Daniel's visions has in earlier Hebrew prophecy is most obvious in the reference to Jeremiah's prophecies in Dan 9:2. There are, however, many allusions to, or echoes of, earlier prophets in Dan 9–12. Nearly every phrase used to describe the messenger in the epiphany vision in Dan 10:5–6 can be found in the descriptions of Ezekiel's visions in Ezek 1; 10. In Ezek 7:20–24 the Israelites are condemned because they have made their own 'abominable images' (v. 20) and so 'profaned' (v. 22) the sacred place. Therefore, YHWH will send enemies who will destroy 'the arrogance of the strong' and inherit their 'houses/temples' (v. 24). Fishbane (1988: 494) points out that the Hebrew roots used here for 'abominable images', 'profane' and 'house/temple' are all used in Dan 11:31 of the action of Antiochus IV against the temple in Jerusalem. The phrase 'the arrogance of the strong' echoes the reference to Israel's pride in the curse formula in Lev 26:19a, which introduces the covenant curses which we have seen lie behind the prayer in Dan 9:4–19.

Fishbane (1988: 490) also argues that Isa 10:22–23; 28:15–22, both oracles about Assyria and the devastation she will cause in Judah as an agent for YHWH's wrath, are alluded to in Dan 11. The verb *šṭp* ('to overflow, sweep away') which occurs in these oracles is used several times in Dan 11 to give the idea of military onslaught (vv. 10, 22, 26, 40). The phrase about a decreed end/destruction in Isa 10:23, 28:22 is echoed in Dan 11:36b, where it is combined with the reference to God's wrath in Isa 10:25. These passages from Isaiah may also be behind the reference to a 'decreed end' in Dan 9:27.

The phrase 'an end at the time appointed' in Dan 11:27b seems to echo Hab 2:3a, 'there is a vision for the appointed time; it speaks of the end'.

What is interesting about the number of these allusions or echoes, and others have been proposed, is that there is nothing like this in the other books of the prophets in the Hebrew Bible. Daniel stands in the tradition of the Hebrew prophets but uses this tradition in a new way, apparently seeing these prophecies as relevant to the events of which Daniel is speaking.

The nature of the prophecies in the dreams and visions in Daniel is different from that in the prophetic books in 'The Prophets'. They are presented as long-range prophecies which are quite detailed, indeed very detailed in Dan 11, and specific chronological information is given. In the classical prophets, God speaks into a specific historical and social situation with a message that is relevant to that time and place. Only very rarely are signs and dates given, and when they are (e.g. Isa 7:10–17; Hag 2:15–19) they refer to the imminent future. Where there is reference to the more distant future, or 'the Day of YHWH' or 'the End', the purpose is to elicit a response with regard to living in the current situation. Daniel is told to seal up his visions until 'the time of the end' (12:4).

In Daniel the term 'prophet' is never used, not even to describe Daniel. The best answer to the question whether Daniel and its eponymous hero belong with the Hebrew prophets seems to be, 'yes and no'. They stand in the tradition of the prophets and have much in common with them, but there are also distinct differences. Many of the differences are shared with another type of literature which became popular with Jews, and then Christians, in the period 250 BCE–250 CE. This is the 'apocalypse'.

Excursus 1: The 'Seventy Sevens' of Daniel 9:20–27

There is general agreement among commentators that the phrase 'seventy sevens/weeks' means 'seventy weeks of years' by analogy with the 'seven weeks of years' in Lev 25:8.

These few verses of Daniel have provoked a vast amount of literature and debate over the centuries. Unfortunately, much of it has been polemical and divisive. As noted in the Preface, the Fifth Monarchists of the seventeenth century used them in their polemic against the English monarchy and establishment. Sir Isaac Newton was only one of many Protestant scholars who used them as part of a strong anti-Roman Catholic polemic in the seventeenth and eighteen centuries. In the nineteenth and twentieth centuries they featured in the 'dispensationalist' debates, that sometimes caused deep divisions in the Evangelical wing of the church, particularly in the Free Churches. Montgomery (1927: 390–401) provides a survey of interpretations prior to 1926 and 'the trackless wilderness of assumptions and theories' that some of them involved. This can be supplemented by the later discussions by Baldwin (1978: 172–8) and A. Y. Collins (in Collins, 1993: 112–23).

Most scholars have assumed that Dan 9:24–27 is intended as a strict chronology of events. A major problem for all attempts to interpret them in this way is in deciding the point at which that chronology begins, 'the time that the word went out to restore and rebuild Jerusalem' (v. 25). The possibilities that have been used are (with dates BCE given first):

605 Jeremiah's prophecy in Jer 25:12.
597 The first deportation referred to in Jer 29:10.
594? The sending of Jeremiah's 'Letter to the Exiles' (Jer 29).
586/7 Jeremiah's prophecies of restoration in Jer 30:18–22; 31:38–40.
539? Gabriel's own words to Daniel.
539 Cyrus' decree recorded in Ezra 1:1–4.
521 Darius' decree recorded in Ezra 6:1–12.
458 Artaxerxes' decree recorded in Ezra 7:12–26.
445 Artaxerxes' warrant given to Nehemiah in Neh 2:7–8.

One issue in the debate is whether the use of the term 'word' in Dan 9:25, rather than a more specific term for a royal decree, indicates that a prophetic 'word of YHWH' is what is meant. Another is the fact that only Jeremiah's prophecies of restoration and Artaxerxes' warrant to Nehemiah actually mention the rebuilding of Jerusalem.

It is possible to distinguish two main lines of chronological interpretation of the 'seventy weeks of years'. They can be labelled the 'messianic' and the 'Maccabean' approaches. Each has a number of variants within it.

The messianic interpretation appears in Christian exegesis towards the end of the second century. It was encouraged by the translation of v. 25 in the dominant Greek translation of Daniel (by Theodotion). This has 'until Christ the chief, seven weeks and sixty-two weeks', which prompted Christian exegetes to take them as a unit and see the coming of Jesus as the end-point of this period of sixty-nine 'weeks of years'. Another factor was that, from Josephus on, Jewish scholars had tended to see the culmination of the weeks in the Roman destruction of Jerusalem by Titus, or sometimes Hadrian. In modern times the starting point of the chronology has been taken as either Artaxerxes' commission to Ezra in 458 or his warrant to Nehemiah in 445. The former date has the problem that the commission does not mention the rebuilding of Jerusalem. Its advantage, however, is that 483 years (69×7) later (remembering that there is no 'year 0' at the turn of the eras) comes to 26 CE, a possible date for the beginning of Jesus' public ministry. His death in 30 CE (a possible, though disputed, date) is taken to occur in the middle of the final week, fulfilment of the rest of the week being postponed into the indefinite future. Starting the chronology at 445, when permission *was* given to rebuild Jerusalem leads to the problem that 483 years later comes to 39 CE. This is 'solved' by postulating that the years of the prophecy are 'prophetic years' of 360 days only, bringing the date down to 32 CE. This is taken as the date of Jesus' death with the fulfilment of the whole of the last week postponed into the indefinite future. At various times and places in the ancient Near-East calendars with twelve months of thirty days were used. However, it was always recognized that these ran out of step with the 'real world' and various methods of intercalary days or months were used to correct for this. It is unlikely that anyone would use these 'short years' in chronological calculations.

Besides these chronological problems the 'messianic' approach faces other problems.

1 In context, 'the word' in v. 25 is most likely to refer to the prophecies of Jeremiah. It is pondering these that leads to Daniel's prayer and Gabriel's visit and revelation.

2 There seems to be no point in saying, 'seven weeks and sixty-two weeks' unless something is going to happen after the seven.

3 The need to introduce an indefinite 'time chasm' either before or in the middle of the last week when nothing in the text suggests it. Also, Konkel (1997: 21) points to the unusual masculine plural ending of 'weeks' here. He argues that where a noun can occur with both plural endings, the feminine form indicates the individual parts of a group and the masculine ending indicates a plurality which forms one total quantity. He therefore insists that the seventy weeks here should be understood as a single, continuous period.

4   The absence of any clear 'messianic' figure elsewhere in Daniel. Even here, in vv. 25–26 the reference is to 'an anointed prince/one' not, as in some English translations, 'the anointed prince/one'. Moreover, they are probably two different figures.

The Maccabean interpretation takes the last week of the seventy to include the period of the persecution of the Jews by Antiochus IV Epiphanes in 167–64 BCE. It is implied by 1 Macc 1:54, where the 'desolating sacrilege' is probably an allusion to Dan 9:27. Porphyry, a pagan opponent of Christianity, argued for it towards the end of the third century CE and so did a Christian scholar, Julius Hilarianus, a century later. Reaction to Porphyry probably contributed to its neglect until modern times. Recent versions of this approach take 'the word' of v. 25 to be one of Jeremiah's prophecies. The 'anointed prince/leader' of v. 25 who comes at the end of first seven weeks is then identified with one of the prominent figures involved in the initial return from exile in Babylon: Cyrus (called 'his [YHWH's] anointed in Isa 45:1); Zerubbabel (the civil leader), or Joshua (the High Priest), who are both called 'sons of oil' in Zech 4:14. There were indeed about 49 (7×7) years between the second deportation in 586/7 and the initial return in 539/8. The 'anointed one' who is 'cut off' after a further sixty-two weeks (v. 26) is identified with the High Priest Onias III who was assassinated by pro-Hellenists in 171. The middle of the final week then falls in 167, the year Antiochus desecrated the Jerusalem Temple and proscribed the Jewish religion. The week ends in 164 when Judas Maccabeus cleansed and rededicated the Temple and Antiochus died unexpectedly. The strength of this approach is that it avoids the exegetical objections to the 'messianic' approach and provides plausible referents for many of the allusions in the prophecy.

The major problem of the 'Maccabean' interpretation is that the period between the initial return from exile and the murder of Onias III is only 367 years, not 434 years (62×7). This is usually explained as the result of prophecy being a 'prophecy after the event' and the author having only a vague knowledge of the chronology of the Persian period. However, Laato (1990) has shown that Jewish writers may not have been as ignorant of, or mistaken about, this chronology as is often claimed.

A symbolic interpretation of the numbers and time periods of Dan 9:24–27 has been advocated by a few modern commentators (e.g. Goldingay, 2019: 484–5; Lucas, 2002: 247–8; Newsom, 2014: 303–4; Pace, 2008: 298–9). Commentators generally understand Jeremiah's use of seventy years for the exile as symbolic, meaning a life-time (Ps 90:10). This makes sense in the context of his 'Letter to the Exiles' (Jer 29) and statement that the exile would last for three generations (Jer 27:7). A different, and deeply symbolic, understanding of the seventy years is expressed in 2 Chr 36:19–23. Here the period from the destruction of Jerusalem and the Temple to the first return is related to the need for the land to make up its lost sabbaths. This implies that the number is being understood symbolically, in the light of the laws about sabbath years (Lev 25:1–7), as ten sabbatical cycles, a 'complete' period of rest for the land. The possible allusion to Lev 25:8 in Dan 9:24 and the verbal links noted above between Daniel's prayer and Lev 26:27–45, a passage which warns of a period of divine wrath measured in sabbatical cycles, makes a symbolic meaning of the 'seventy weeks' in terms of sabbatical cycles probable.

In the Hebrew Bible the number seven is often associated with completeness and perfection. This is even more true of the number seventy. Seventy weeks of years, then, signifies a complete period, the one needed to bring in the perfect kingdom (v. 24). This period (490 years) is also ten jubilee cycles. Jubilee is the main theme of Lev 25, the passage from which the concept of 'weeks of years' is taken. The jubilee year was the great year of release: from debt and slavery, and restoration of family lands. Therefore, a period of ten jubilee cycles is an appropriate period to symbolize the coming of the ultimate act of divine deliverance and restoration. As noted above, the first seven weeks (49 years) corresponds fairly well with one way of measuring the exile chronologically, but the figure is probably used because it represents the years that lead up to a year of jubilee, of release for slaves and captives. The antithesis of perfection is sometimes represented by one less than the perfect number, as in the number 666 as the number of the beast in Rev 13:18. So, it is appropriate that the climax of devastation comes at the end of the sixty-ninth week. The period of sixty-two weeks is then simply the inevitable result of subtracting the first symbolic period (seven weeks) from the second (sixty-nine weeks). One week of seven years is a suitable symbolic period for evil to reach its climax and be brought to a total end. It just so happens that the murder of Onias III and the rededication of the Temple are separated by about this period and that the desecration of the Temple comes, very approximately, in the middle of it.

If this symbolic approach to the 'seventy sevens' is accepted, it means that they should not be read as an attempt at a chronological scheme of history but as an example of what has come to be called a 'chronography'. This is a symbolic scheme of history which is intended to interpret the major events within it, not as providing a means of predicting when they will happen.

Grabbe (1979) has argued that this is a feature of Hellenistic Jewish historiography. This way of reading of Dan 9:24–27 can be combined with the way the Maccabean approach identifies the characters and events alluded to. Its purpose is to provide a way of understanding these events as divine acts of deliverance and restoration.

Daniel and apocalyptic

The publication in 1821 of *1 Enoch*, which is contained in the Bible of the Ethiopic Church, led to a discussion of the similarities between the books of *Daniel*, *1 Enoch*, the *Sibylline Oracles*, *4 Ezra* and *Revelation* (titled *Apocalypse of John* in some Greek manuscripts). During the rest of the nineteenth century and the early twentieth century several books were discovered, or rediscovered, which had similarities to these books, such as *2 & 3 Apocalypse of Baruch*, *Apocalypse of Abraham*, *Assumption (Testament) of Moses*, *2 Enoch* and *Jubilees*. Because a number of these books had 'apocalypse' in their title this corpus was called 'apocalyptic literature'. Scholars began to identify apocalyptic literature in the Hebrew Bible and New Testament apart from *Daniel* and *Revelation*, most notably Isa 24–27 and Mark 13. Isaiah 56–66, Ezekiel and Zechariah also became subjects of debate in this respect.

During the first half of the twentieth century scholars tried to isolate what the common features are that define the corpus of apocalypses. Some emphasized aspects of their literary form, others looked more to their content, including important theological themes. There is considerable diversity within the corpus. One response to this was to take a particular book, commonly *Revelation*, as a standard for comparison. It did not help that, as scholars debated what influence the apocalypses and the way of thought they represent might have had on Second Temple Judaism and early Christianity, terms such as 'apocalypse' and especially 'apocalyptic' came to be used by different people with varying meanings and without clear definition.

The confused nature of the debate is captured in the original German title of an influential book by Koch published in 1970, *Ratlos vor der Apokalyptik, Helpless/Perplexed Before Apocalyptic* (English edition: Koch, 1972). Koch insisted that a distinction must be made between the literary genre 'apocalypse' and the historical 'apocalyptic' movement from which it arose. In his view it was necessary to have a clear definition of the literary genre before attempting to understand the parent movement. He followed the tradition of listing a set of what he saw as key characteristics of apocalypses.

1 Discourse cycles centred on visions and/or auditions.
2 Paraenetic (exhortatory) discourses.
3 Use of symbolic, often mythical, imagery.
4 A description of the seer's spiritual turmoils.
5 Composite in character.
6 Pseudonymity.

Koch did not claim that all these elements are found in all apocalypses, but saw them as indicating the common core of the genre. Hanson (1976) proposed a refinement of Koch's approach. He made a threefold distinction between apocalypse (the literary genre), apocalyptic eschatology (a religious perspective) and apocalypticism (a religio-social movement).

A seminar was set up by the Society of Biblical Literature (SBL) to produce a definition of the literary genre 'apocalypse'. It surveyed a considerable number of works normally accepted as apocalypses from the period 250 BCE to 250 CE. These included Jewish pseudepigraphical and rabbinic works, Christian, gnostic, Graeco-Roman and Persian works. The definition they produced (Collins, 1979) lists the following as characteristic of the genre.

1 It is revelatory literature with a narrative framework.
2 A revelation is given to a human recipient through a being from another, supernatural, world.
3 The revelation discloses a transcendent reality.
4 This reality has a temporal aspect in that it includes eschatological salvation.
5 It has a spatial aspect in that it involves another, supernatural, world.

The seminar found that personal afterlife is the most consistent feature of the eschatology of the apocalypses. It also concluded that apocalypses fall into two sub-genres: those with surveys of history and those with otherworldly journeys (only the *Apocalypse of Abraham* includes both). This definition doesn't seek to do more than cover the core characteristics of apocalypses. They may also include other literary forms, such as the paraenetic discourses listed by Koch and prayers, since most apocalypses are, as he said, composites of different types of literature.

This definition has been the subject of discussion and debate. Some, like Rowland (1982: 14, 29–37, 71), have questioned the inclusion of eschatology in it, for two reasons. First, it is pointed out that there is some diversity in the eschatology of the apocalypses. It is true that only those with a survey of history present an 'end of history' scenario of some kind. All of them, however, do have an eschatology that involves retribution beyond death. This diversity is not really any greater than the diversity in the forms of vision reports. The second reason given is that neither the idea of 'the end of history' nor of judgement beyond death is restricted to the apocalypses. However, the same can be said of visions and heavenly journeys. The SBL genre definition seeks to identify a combination of features which make the genre 'apocalypse' distinctive. Some of these are found in other genres, though it is worth noting that judgement after death is a major difference between the eschatology of the Hebrew prophets and that of the apocalypses. Hellholm (1986) and others have raised a different issue. They argue that the definition should include a reference to the purpose and social setting of the apocalypses. This is usually seen as giving encouragement and/or consolation to a group facing some kind of crisis. This runs contrary to Koch's insistence, noted above, that it is necessary to have a clear definition of the genre before trying to understand the historical movement from which it arose. Without this, the reconstruction of the historical social setting can become very subjective. There is also a danger of having a too narrow and fixed view of the probable social setting of the apocalypses. Despite these criticisms the SBL definition has been widely accepted as a working definition for the genre 'apocalypse'.

There has been, and still is, much debate about the origins of apocalyptic. For much of the twentieth century there was a considerable consensus that the main root of it was the Hebrew prophets. This was challenged by von Rad (1965: 301–8), who argued that the roots of apocalyptic were to be found in the wisdom traditions. His main argument was that the apocalypses present the course of history as determined, whereas the Hebrew prophets do not. The line of continuity that he saw between wisdom and apocalyptic lay in the fact that part of wisdom is to know the time for everything. He also pointed to the fact that the apocalyptists often refer to themselves as scribes and that the apocalypses seem to be the product of purely literary activity not the recording of what was originally oral proclamation. His proposal has not found much support in the form in which he presented it. Müller (1972), however, modified it and developed it. He emphasized that ancient Near Eastern wisdom contains both didactic and divinatory (often called 'mantic') strands, and argued that one, though not the only, root of apocalyptic was mantic wisdom. There is no evidence of a class of mantic wise men in Israel or Judah, but two godly Hebrews, Joseph and Daniel, do act in that role in pagan courts. They have the gift of interpreting symbolic dreams and visions. Müller's proposal has been received more positively than von Rad's. It has led to growing interest in, and recognition of, the influence of Mesopotamian mantic wisdom on the development of apocalyptic. There are other possible sources of influence on the thought and imagery of the apocalypses that have been included in the debate: Persian, especially Zoroastrian, thought with its dualism and eschatology; Babylonian and Canaanite mythology; Hellenistic ideas. We shall refer to some of these when discussing the imagery in Daniel's visions in ch. 3.

How does Daniel relate to the apocalypses? As a whole, the book does not fit well into the SBL definition. There is no real parallel to the stories in Dan 1–6 in the apocalypses. The dreams and visions in them do not involve an otherworldly interpreter. Daniel interprets them thanks to wisdom given by God. The stories do not give a framework to the visions in Dan 7–12 but act as a prelude to them. The visions in Dan 7, 8 and 9 do each have a narrative framework, and involve an otherworldly interpreter. It is debatable whether those in Dan 8 and 9 envisage eschatological salvation. None of these three visions mention personal afterlife, which the SBL Seminar found to be the most consistent feature of the eschatology of the apocalypses. The one part of Daniel that does fit the SBL definition is Dan 10–12. It is the only place in the Hebrew Bible where there is a clear statement of personal afterlife, and this includes judgement and resurrection. It clearly fits into the sub-genre of 'historical' apocalypses because of its long and detailed survey of history in ch. 11.

Where does Daniel fit in the development of the apocalypses? The earliest apocalypses are found in *1 Enoch*. This is a composite work and two of its parts, the Book of Watchers and the Astronomical Book, which are apocalypses with otherworldly journeys, come from the early second or even late third century BCE. They therefore pre-date the visions in Dan 7–12 if these come from about the mid-second century BCE, but are further removed from Hebrew Prophets than they are (Collins, 1998: 25). One would not expect a genre, especially a complex one, to suddenly appear fully formed. A period of development and experimentation would be understandable before the genre settled into a 'normal' form. Daniel and these early Enochic compositions seem to belong to an early period in the development of the apocalypse as a genre. The combination of stories and visions in Daniel does not have any clear precedent and does not become a feature of the genre. On the other hand, Daniel has resurrection as part of its eschatology, which becomes a feature of most historical apocalypses.

Excursus 2: The survey of history in Daniel 11

There is no precedent in the Hebrew prophets for the long, detailed survey of history found in Dan 11. Despite its terse, enigmatic wording it is not difficult to identify the main historical events to which it alludes, except at the beginning and at the end.

We will discuss the identity of 'Darius the Mede' in ch. 5, but in the light of Dan 5:31 the reference in Dan 11:1 is to the fall of Babylon to Cyrus the Great. The problem in Dan11:2 is that it seems to be referring to rulers of Persia who will follow Cyrus, and there were thirteen of them from Cyrus the Great to Darius III. So, who are the four mentioned in this verse? Since the time of Jerome some have argued that the reference is to the four kings who followed Cyrus: Cambyses, Smerdis, Darius I and Xerxes I. This has the advantage that Xerxes I was renowned for his wealth and he invaded Greece. In his day it was not a kingdom, it only became one under Philip of Macedon in 338 BCE, but a collection of city states. He was defeated at the Battle of Salamis in 480 BCE. However, there is a long gap of well over a century between Xerxes I and the fall of the Persian Empire. Other scholars have pointed out that only four Persian rulers are mentioned in the Hebrew Bible (Ezra 4:5–7): Cyrus, Darius, Ahasuerus (Xerxes) and Artaxerxes. They assume that these are in mind here. This raises the problem of the identity of the wealthy fourth king, who clashes with Greece. They suggest that he is the last Persian king, Darius III, with the 'wealth' being that accumulated by the Persian Empire. A few commentators have taken a different approach to understanding the verse. They note that the wording, 'three ... and then a fourth' is an idiom (a 'graded numerical saying') used in wisdom sayings (e.g. see Prov 30:15b–31) and which is used in a series of oracles of judgement in Amos 1–2. It seems to indicate the giving of examples that fully represent the nature of something. Here use of the idiom would be a way of summarizing the nature of the Persian kings as rulers who amass wealth, grow strong and provoke conflict with Greece. Given the probable links of apocalyptic with the wisdom traditions, this is a reasonable suggestion.

11:3. The victorious career of Alexander the Great, 336–323 BCE.

11:4. His death and the division of his empire among his successors.

11:5. In 323 Ptolemy gained control of Egypt, and also Palestine including Judea, and founded the Ptolemaic dynasty. He is 'the king of the south'. Seleucus gained control of Babylon but fled to Egypt in 316 when attacked by Antigonus, the ruler of Asia Minor. He became one of Ptolemy's generals. Together they defeated Antigonus at the Battle of Gaza in 312. Seleucus then regained Babylon, founding the Seleucid dynasty. After Antigonus' death in the Battle of Ipsus in 301, he gradually took over his territory and extended his realm until it was the largest of the successor kingdoms of Alexander's empire.

11:6. In about 250, Antiochus II, the 'king of the north', grandson of Seleucus I, divorced his wife Laodice and made a marriage alliance with Ptolemy II by marrying his daughter Berenice, by whom he had a son. After two years he was reconciled to Laodice. Shortly after this he died and she arranged the murder of Berenice, her son, and her Egyptian attendants.

11:7–9. This refers to hostilities between Ptolemy III, brother of Berenice, and Seleucus II, son of Laodice, over control of Palestine.

11:10. Seleucus II was succeeded by his son, Seleucus III (226–223), whose reign was cut short by his murder while campaigning in Asia Minor. His brother, Antiochus III succeeded him. When Ptolemy IV, a weak character, came to the throne in 222 Antiochus saw the opportunity to regain territory in Syria lost by his father. He then pushed further south.

11:11–19. These verses cover the career of Antiochus III. After an initial defeat by Ptolemy IV in southern Palestine he made peace with him. Antiochus then extended his control in Asia Minor and central Asia. His successes here led to his title 'Antiochus the Great'. When Ptolemy IV and his queen died in 204 his son, Ptolemy V, was an infant. Increasing unrest in Egypt led Antiochus to move against the country. He eventually gained control of Palestine in 198 (v. 16). He then made a marriage alliance with Ptolemy V, giving him his daughter Cleopatra to be his wife. She, however, eventually encouraged her husband to make an alliance with Rome against her father (v. 17). Despite the peace treaty Antiochus took over areas on the coast of Asia Minor held by Egypt and then attacked Greece. This led to intervention by the Romans. They drove him back east of the Taurus Mountains. After a crushing defeat by Lucius Scipio at the Battle of Magnesia in 190 Antiochus had to accept humiliating terms in the Treaty of Apamea in 188, including paying a large indemnity (v. 18). He was killed in 187 while trying to rob the treasury of the temple of Bel in Elymais (v. 19).

11:20. Antiochus the Great's younger son, Antiochus, was a hostage in Rome. His elder son, Seleucus IV succeeded him on the throne. He inherited his father's great debts. This verse refers to the abortive attempt of his prime minister, Heliodorus, to rob the treasury of the temple in Jerusalem (2 Macc. 3). Seleucus IV was assassinated in 175.

11:21. This reflects the machinations which accompanied the rise to power of Antiochus IV, later known as 'Antiochus Epiphanes'. Shortly before his death Seleucus sent his eldest son, Demetrius, to Rome as a hostage in place of Antiochus. On his death Heliodorus claimed the throne, ostensibly as Regent for Seleucus' younger son, Antiochus. Antiochus, who was on his way home from Rome, arrived with an army and Heliodorus fled. Antiochus assumed the throne as Antiochus IV, supposedly as co-regent with his nephew Antiochus on behalf of his older nephew Demetrius. The younger nephew was murdered in 170.

11:22-24. Many commentators see this as a general depiction of the character of Antiochus IV and the nature of his reign. Some try to relate it specifically to his dealings with the Jews.

11:25-30. When Ptolemy V died his queen, Cleopatra, acted as Regent for her young son Ptolemy VI. He was still a youth when she died. Powerful courtiers encouraged him to try to regain control of Palestine. These verses refer to the resulting hostilities, which involved two campaigns against Egypt by Antiochus IV, and were complicated by factionalism within Egypt which for a while saw both Ptolemy VI and his younger brother Ptolemy VII claiming to be king. According to 1 Macc 1:20-28, on his way home after the first campaign in 169 Antiochus robbed the temple in Jerusalem. During the second campaign in 168 Rome, to whom Egypt had appealed for help, intervened. An envoy from the Roman Senate confronted Antiochus outside Alexandria demanding his immediate withdrawal from Egypt. Antiochus complied (v. 30a). On his way home, hearing of in-fighting in Jerusalem, he sent an army to attack the city (v. 30b).

11:31–35. These verses refer to Antiochus' proscription of the Jewish religion and his persecution of those who remained faithful to it during 167–164. This will be discussed in some detail later.

11:36–39. This is a summary and evaluation of Antiochus' character and policies. The general statement in v. 36 is expanded in the following verses.

11:40–45. Although this section seems to continue the story of Antiochus, leading up to his expected downfall and death, most scholars are not convinced by attempts (e.g. by House, 2018: 178–9) to correlate them with the known events following his withdrawal from Egypt in 168 until his death in 164. Four different accounts of his final campaign and death are given in 1 Macc 6:1–17; 2 Macc 1:11–17; 9:1–29; and Polybius (*Hist.* 31.9). Despite their differences, they all agree that Antiochus set out on a campaign in Persia, failed in an attempt to rob a temple and met an untimely death. Three of them say he died of a sudden illness. A Babylonian king list shows that his death was known in Babylon in December 164 BCE.

3

Daniel: The Wise Man

Investigation

Read Job 26:7–13; Ps 74:12–17; 89:8–12. The context of these passages makes clear that the writers are referring to the creation of the cosmos. In Isa 51:9–11 the prophet conflates the creation of the cosmos with the story of the exodus from Egypt in an oracle promising a new exodus from captivity in Babylon. Can you construct an outline of the creation story alluded to in these passages?

An oracle in Isa 27:1 looks forward to an ultimate destruction of the power of evil in the cosmos.

Do you think these passages throw any light on the imagery used in the vision in Dan 7:1–13 and its interpretation?

Introduction

Daniel and his friends are never portrayed as typical Hebrew prophets in the book of Daniel. It is clear from Dan 2:10 that they are counted among the 'wise men' in the court of Nebuchadnezzar. Indeed, Daniel is appointed as the chief of these wise men (Dan 2:48; 5:11). These were not wise men of the kind who produced proverbial wisdom such as is found in the Hebrew books of Proverbs and Ecclesiastes. The lists given in Dan 2:2; 27 indicate what kind of expertise these wise men had: magicians, enchanters, sorcerers, Chaldeans and diviners. These are experts in what Müller called 'mantic wisdom', the use of techniques of divination and the interpretation of the resulting omens. The meaning of some of the terms is not certain but a general consensus is given below. The first four are Hebrew words from Dan 2:2 and the last is an Aramaic word from Dan 2:27.

Magicians	ḥarṭummîm	Dream interpreters.
Enchanters	'aššapîm	Interpreters of signs in people who are ill.
Sorcerers	məkaššəpîm	Users of charms and incantations.
Chaldeans	kaśdîm	Here this is not an ethnic term but refers to astrologers.
Diviners	gazərîn	Exorcists (probably).

Apart from the High Priestly use of Urim and Thummim, which seems to have been a technique for getting a yes/no answer to a question, and is not mentioned after the reign of King David, of all the means of divination used in the ancient Near East only dreams and dream interpretation have an acceptable place within orthodox Hebrew religion in the Hebrew Bible. In the court stories Daniel is renowned for his ability to interpret dreams and visions. He, however, does not consult books of dream omens but relies on revelation from his God (Dan 2:17–19, 27).

Wise men in the king's court had to be literate. That is why Nebuchadnezzar commanded that the Judean exiles who had been selected as potential courtiers, including Daniel and his friends, should be 'taught the literature and language of the Chaldeans', an education that would take three years (Dan 1:3–6). In the Hebrew Bible outside Daniel the term 'Chaldean' is used in an ethnic sense of the people of Babylonia in general, as it is in Dan 5:30; 9:1. It may have that sense here since the language that the Judean exiles would be taught was Babylonian which, like Assyrian, was a dialect of the Akkadian language. However, they would learn it as part of a course preparing them to be courtiers. In the fifth century BCE Herodotus (*Hist.* 1.181–3) uses the term 'Chaldean' in a restricted sense as referring to a priestly tribe or caste. In Hellenistic times the term is used of experts in astrology and astrological omens. So, it is probable that here it is being used as a way of referring to wise men in general.

The primary writing material used in Mesopotamia was a tablet made of soft clay. Scribes wrote on it using a stylus which was usually made from the stem of a reed. After it had been left to dry in the sun the tablet was robust. The end of the stylus, which struck the clay first, made a wider mark than its stem, resulting in a wedge-shaped impression from which this writing system gets its modern name: cuneiform, derived from the Latin *cuneus* ('wedge'). The characters, or signs, used in writing Akkadian were groups of wedge-shaped marks and each represented a syllable, a combination of a vowel and consonant(s). Because many such combinations are possible a syllabic system requires many more characters than an alphabetic system which uses one character for each vowel and consonant. Moreover, in the Akkadian syllabary most consonants are represented by more than one sign, some by several. As a result, the complete syllabary consists of about six hundred signs. The need to learn so many signs and their meanings, how to write them and then how to use them to represent words, contributed to the length of time taken to be trained as a wise man. In the latter part of the training to use the cuneiform writing system the students copied out a corpus of classic religious and literary texts, hence the reference to 'the literature and language of the Chaldeans' in Dan 1:8. This meant that the course was also an induction into the religion and culture of Babylon.

If the picture of Daniel and his friends as Babylonian-trained wise men given in the stories in Daniel provides us with a guide to the kind of people who were the authors of the book it may help us understand some of the features which make it distinctive within the Hebrew Bible. It might help to explain the use of strange, at times even bizarre, imagery in some of the dreams and visions, and the use of forms of literature not found elsewhere in the Hebrew Bible. These features may have their roots in Mesopotamian, or wider ancient Near Eastern, culture, literature and religion.

Daniel: The courtier

Daniel 2: Nebuchadnezzar's dream of a statue

Some scholars suggest that in this chapter an original story about an unnamed Jewish exile has been taken and adapted to make it one about Daniel. They point to three pieces of evidence for this. The first is the clash between the date in v. 1 and the reference to three years of training for Daniel and his friends in Dan 1:5. Secondly, there is the strange absence of Daniel and his friends from the gathering of wise men in v. 2, implied by v. 15. Finally, there is the confusion that in v. 16 Daniel goes to see the king yet in v. 25 Arioch introduces him to the king as if he is someone unknown to Nebuchadnezzar, contrary to what one might expect in the light of Dan 1:19–20. Suggestions have been made for resolving some of these points. Driver (1900: 17) argued that the dating issue might arise from different ways of reckoning time in the ancient Neat East. In the Babylonian reckoning of kings' reigns, their accession year, whatever its length, was 'year zero' and therefore Nebuchadnezzar's second year would be the third chronological year of his reign. The three years of training in Dan 1:5 might be reckoned according to the Hebrew method in which parts of a year are counted as a full year, so that a period of two years spread over three chronological years becomes three years (cf. 2 Kgs 18:9–10). This proposal requires that Nebuchadnezzar captured Jerusalem in his accession year, a problematic issue which will be discussed in ch. 5 in relation to Dan 1:1–2. Goldingay (2019: 178, 198) questions whether v. 16 actually implies that Daniel really saw the king. He may have had his request granted by a highly placed official.

It may be, however, that this kind of debate about consistency and historical accuracy in the story is not appropriate with regard to a court story like this one. In Chapter 1 it was argued that these stories, whatever their basis in an actual event, were not written as historical reports but to entertain, educate and encourage. The writers used their literary skills to achieve those ends. Whatever 'historical' reason there may or may not be for the absence of Daniel and his friends from the council in v. 2 (and one can think of various possibilities) in literary terms it is very important. It sets up the whole conflict that is the centre of the story. The writer is not interested in explaining whatever procedures Daniel might have needed to go through in v. 16. That would slow up the narrative in an unhelpful way. Arioch's description of Daniel in v. 25b is important to the story because it underlines the central issue, the contrast between the failure of the Babylonian wise men and Daniel, a Judean exile. It prepares the way for the theologically important opening of his speech in vv. 27–28. This seems as plausible an explanation of these apparent anomalies as attributing them to oversights or errors by a redactor of the story.

It has also been suggested that the interpretation is either an adaptation or replacement of an original one. This is because in places it contains details that are different from what is said in the description of the dream. Most notably there is the reference to toes in vv. 41–42, which are not mentioned in the description of the dream and whereas in the dream 'a stone was cut out, not by human hands', struck the statue and then became a great mountain

(vv. 34–35), in the interpretation 'a stone was cut from the mountain not by hand' (v. 45). In response to this it has been pointed out that such repetition with variation is a feature of the book of Daniel. We have noted it already in the lists of the wise men in chs 2 and 5. Perhaps most significantly it is also seen in the interpretation of the vision in Dan 7:19–22, in which the fourth beast gains 'claws of bronze' but the eyes of the little horn are not said to be 'like human eyes' as in the vision report.

The imagery in Nebuchadnezzar's dream, a statue and the symbolic use of different metals, has no precedent in the Hebrew Bible. In the eighth century BCE the Greek poet Hesiod divides history into five eras, four of them symbolized by the metals, gold, silver, bronze and iron. Between the eras of bronze and iron he inserts the era of the Greek heroes, without using any metal to symbolize it (*Works and Days*, 109–201). In the early first century CE the Latin poet Ovid (*Metamorphoses*, 1.89–162) uses the four-metal scheme without the era of the heroes. This scheme seems to be based on the historical memory of the transition from the bronze age to the iron age. When describing the era of bronze Hesiod comments that at that time humans had only bronze implements because there was no iron. A similar scheme of four ages symbolized by four metals is found in two Zoroastrian texts: *Denkard* 9.8 and *Zand-I Vohuman Ysn* 1 (also known as *Bahaman Yasht*). Zoroastrianism was a religion founded by Zarathushtra which took root in Persia. In these texts Zarathushtra has a dream in which he sees a tree with branches of gold, silver, steel and 'iron mixed' (the exact meaning of this term is unknown). The texts are known only from manuscripts of the thirteenth century CE and later and the dating of the material in them is a much-debated problem. The rulers of the final age are described as '*divs* with dishevelled hair'. The word *divs* means 'evil spirits' but here it seems to be used in a metaphorical, derogatory, sense. It probably refers to Alexander the Great and his successors. On coins and sculptures Alexander is always depicted with dishevelled hair, whereas in the reliefs in Persepolis the Persian king and courtiers always have well-groomed hair. This strongly suggests that in its present form the scheme in these texts is no older than the Hellenistic period. The origin of the scheme could, of course, be earlier than this.

It is often suggested that imagery of four empires symbolized by metals in Dan 2 has its origin in Zoroastrian sources because the motif of 'iron mixed with clay' is assumed to be derived from the 'iron mixed' of the Zoroastrian texts. This view, however, is problematic. The dating of the sources is a matter of debate, and so is the dating of the penetration of Zoroastrianism into western Iran (sixth century BCE?) and its acceptance at the Persian court (see Boyce 1975, 1982). The uncertainty about the meaning of the term 'iron mixed' makes it precarious to assume that it prompted the 'iron mixed with clay' in Dan 2. This could be an adaptation of the scheme found in Hesiod in order to reflect some historical reality about the fourth kingdom, such as the marriage alliances between the Ptolemies and Seleucids which are referred to in Dan 11:6, 17. Since the scheme in Dan 2 is otherwise identical to that in Hesiod and Ovid it is reasonable to conclude with Collins (1974: 11) that it is derived from a scheme widely known in the eastern Mediterranean world and used by these two poets rather than from a Persian source. Since this scheme has a historical basis, it is likely that the Zoroastrian scheme is an adaptation of it. The probability that the addition of 'iron mixed with clay' is an original addition by the author if Dan 2 is supported by the fact that the motif of the stone that fills the earth has no known precedent in non-biblical sources. It has a likely basis in the Hebrew Bible. The phrase 'my/the Rock' is an epithet for YHWH, especially in the Psalms (e.g. Pss 18:2; 42:9; 71:3). The motif of the mountain echoes Isa 2:2–4//Mic 4:1–4 where, when YHWH's rule is established, people say, 'come, let us go up to the mountain of YHWH'. The motif of filling the earth echoes Isa 6:3 (filling with YHWH's glory) and Isa 11:9 (filling with the knowledge of YHWH).

The identification of Nebuchadnezzar as the golden head of the statue has prompted a minority of scholars to interpret the statue in terms of a sequence of individual rulers, with little consensus on who they are. Some have identified them with the four named in the book of Daniel: Nebuchadnezzar, Belshazzar, Darius the Mede and Cyrus the Persian. However, Cyrus is only mentioned three times, and only in passing comments (1:21; 6:28 [MT 29]; 10:1). Most scholars turn to Dan 7–8 as a basis for interpreting the statue of Dan 2. Even if by a different author, they provide the earliest interpretation of this chapter. Although the four beasts of ch. 7 are said to represent four 'kings' (7:17) it is clear that the fourth beast represents a kingdom ruled over by a sequence of eleven kings (7:24). Given this fluidity, the fact that the head is identified with an individual does not require that it, or the other parts of the statue, should refer only to individual kings. The imagery used of the first beast (7:4) echoes that used of Nebuchadnezzar in Dan 4, and there is general agreement that this beast represents the Babylonian Empire. What is said of the 'little horn' that arises from the fourth beast in ch. 7 corresponds with what is said of the 'little horn' that arises from the goat in ch. 8. This strongly suggests that the fourth beast, like the goat, represents the Macedonian Empire of Alexander and its successors. As noted above, this fits with the reference to marriage alliances in 2:43. This leads to the overall sequence of the empires being: Babylonian, Median, Persian, Macedonian. The inclusion of the Median Empire in this sequence is often seen as strange. During its existence it overlapped with the Neo-Babylonian Empire, which out-lived it by a little more than a decade. Unlike it, it never ruled the Jews. We will return to this issue when discussing the interpretation of the vision in Dan 7.

Daniel 4: Nebuchadnezzar's dream and illness

Until the mid-nineteenth century CE 'King Belshazzar' of Babylon was known only from the references to him in Daniel and one in Baruch 1:11, which seems dependent on Daniel. According to classical sources Nabonidus was King of Babylon when it fell to Cyrus, so there seemed no place for Belshazzar among the kings of Babylon. In 1854 some foundation cylinder inscriptions were excavated in the temple of the moon-god Sin in Ur which recorded repair work done by Nabonidus. They end with a prayer for Bel-šarra-uṣur, his son and heir. Other mentions of Belshazzar have subsequently come to light in cuneiform sources. It is now clear that for some ten years of his reign Nabonidus was absent from Babylon, based at Teima in Arabia. During this period Belshazzar acted a Regent in Babylon (Beaulieu, 1989).

Through the twentieth century there was a growing consensus that Nabonidus' absence from Babylon might lie behind the story of Nebuchadnezzar's madness in Dan 4. This gained momentum with the discovery of an Aramaic text at Qumran, the so-called 'Prayer of Nabonidus' (variously designated as 4QPrNab, 4QOrNab, 4Q242; see DJD 22, 83–93). This records that for seven years while he was in Teima Nabonidus suffered from a serious disease. He prayed to the gods of gold, silver, wood, stone and clay but was healed only when a Jewish diviner came to him, who urged him to give honour to the true God. There are clear parallels with Dan 4: a Babylonian king suffers illness for seven years, a Jewish diviner is involved, the king writes a letter to honour God, and the extant narrative is in the first person. There are also clear differences: the king's name is different, as is the illness, and the location, the Jew is unnamed.

Eusebius (*Praep. Ev.* 9.41.6) reports a story which he says he found in a book by Abydenus, *Concerning the Assyrians*, who attributes at least some of it to the Greek author Megasthenes (c. 300 BCE). In this story Nebuchadnezzar, at the height of his power, was walking on the palace roof when he was moved to utter a prophecy that a 'Persian mule' would be aided by the gods of Babylon to enslave the Babylonians. He then expressed the wish that, instead of this, the 'Persian mule' would be driven into the desert to wander with the wild beasts and birds. Again, there are similarities and differences with Dan 4. On the one hand there is the king, the location and the motif of living with the wild beasts. However, in Dan 4 the voice comes from heaven, the 'prophecy' concerns Nebuchadnezzar's own fate, and speaks of him becoming like a beast.

There is a fragmentary cuneiform text that seems to refer to some mental disorder afflicting Nebuchadnezzar, and perhaps to him neglecting and leaving Babylon, and mentions repentance for neglect of the gods (Wiseman, 1985: 102–4; this also includes a translation and discussion of the 'Prayer of Nabonidus').

The existence of the non-biblical traditions about Nebuchadnezzar suggests some caution in transferring the story in Dan 4 to Nabonidus, especially since very little is known about the last thirty years of Nebuchadnezzar's reign. The most that can be concluded with any confidence is that Dan 4 is one of a number of stories about Nebuchadnezzar and Nabonidus which have some elements in common. The literary relationships between them are unclear and probably complex.

The central motif of Nebuchadnezzar's dream is a great tree sited at the centre of the earth which reaches up to heaven and provides food and shelter for all living creatures. This motif is found in many different cultures and religions. Such a tree is often a symbol for the transcendent, sustaining, cosmos – the Cosmic Tree. Although this widespread imagery is a clearly relevant background for the tree in Dan 4, there is probably also dependence on some passages in Ezekiel. In Ezek 17 the Davidic dynasty is depicted as a cedar of Lebanon. Its topmost shoot is broken off and replanted. Ezekiel 17:22–24, which refer to the restoration of Judah from exile, has particular resemblance to Dan 4:11–12. In Ezek 19:10–14 Jerusalem is represented as a towering vine which is plucked up and cast down on the ground, stripped of its fruit and withers. Closest to Dan 4 is Ezek 31, in which Pharaoh is compared to a cedar of Lebanon of great height which gives shelter to all the birds and animals. Because of its pride God let it be cut down. This tree is explicitly linked with the Garden of Eden (v. 9). The Tree of Life in the

Garden of Eden may be behind the reference to the tree providing food for everyone in Dan 4:9. In each of these three passages there is the theme of great splendour leading to great pride, which is then punished by the tree being cut down. This is the theme of Dan 4.

Daniel: The visionary

Daniel 7 and 8: Bizarre beasts

The background of the bizarre bestial imagery of Daniel's vision in 7:1–8 has been the subject of much debate. Attempts have been made to relate the links between animals and nations here, and in ch. 8, with astrological geography. In this, nations are linked with specific stellar constellations that supposedly influence their destiny. However, there is no one scheme that links the nations that are probably referred to in the visions to the relevant animal constellations. Moreover, none of the known schemes are earlier than the first century CE.

In a study of the imagery in Dan 7, Day (1985: 157) concludes that the basis for the four types of animals is Hos 13:7–8. Here YHWH, acting in judgement on Israel, is compared to four beasts (in this order): a lion, a leopard, a bear and an unspecified 'wild beast'. The change in order in Daniel may be explained by the fact that in the Hebrew Bible it is the lion and the bear that are depicted as the two most ferocious beasts and they are occasionally paired because of this (1 Sam 17:34–37; Prov 28:15). This is a plausible conclusion regarding the kinds of beasts depicted but there is no precedent in the Hebrew Bible for the bizarre nature of them in the vision.

Hybrid beasts do appear in Mesopotamian iconography. Animals with wings, especially lions, and/or two or more heads are depicted. Bears, however, are rarely depicted, and then only in the mountainous areas where they live, and there are no known depictions of leopards. Since Gunkel (1895: 323–35, English edition 2006) expounded Dan 7 in the light of the Babylonian creation story *Enūma Eliš* a number of scholars have pointed to it as the source of the imagery of the beasts from the sea. In this story, prior to creating an ordered cosmos, Marduk has to subdue the forces of chaos, symbolized by Ti'amat and her horde of hideous sea monsters. He traps her using the winds of heaven before slaying her. The most obvious parallels with Dan 7 are the motif of monsters in turbulent waters and the reference to the winds of heaven. The name Ti'amat is derived from an Akkadian root meaning 'sea'. There are a number of references in the Hebrew Bible to God quelling monsters or turbulent waters in the beginning, or which he will quell again (e.g. Job 26:13; Pss 74:13–14; 89:9–10; Isa 17:12–13; Isa 27:1; Ezek 29:3–5; 32:2–4). This suggests that a creation story similar to *Enūma Eliš* was known to the biblical writers.

Since the texts from Ugarit have become known most scholars have concluded that where these motifs occur in the Hebrew Bible the source is more likely to be Canaanite than Mesopotamian (e.g. Day, 1985, especially ch. 1). The Ugaritic texts do not contain a creation story. They do contain an account of Baal's defeat of Yam (Sea). They also allude to a defeat of Leviathan (*ltn*, the vowels are not indicated in the script), who has seven heads (cf. Ps 74:14, 'heads of Leviathan') and is described as 'the twisting (*brḥ*) serpent' (cf. Job 26:13; Isa 27:1, '*bāriaḥ* serpent') and 'the crooked (*'qltn*) serpent' (cf. Isa 27:1 '*'ăqallātōn* serpent'). In the Ugaritic texts *ltn* is also called *tnn*, 'dragon', a term identical to *tannîn* mentioned in some biblical passages (e.g. Isa 27:1; 51:9). Although these similarities are striking, the events in the story of Baal's conflict with Yam are very different from those in Dan 7 and it has a different theme: the rivalry and jealousy between two gods. Also, the motifs of the four winds of heaven and beasts rising from the sea are absent.

If Daniel has its origin in Babylonia, it is possible that in the case of Dan 7 the source of the imagery was the Babylonian New Year Festival, of which *Enūma Eliš* was part of the liturgy. A possible indication of direct Babylonian influence is the phrase 'the four winds of heaven' in v. 2. Its only other occurrences in the Hebrew Bible are Dan 8:8; 11:4 and Zech 2:6 [MT 10]. The shorter phrase 'the four winds' occurs in Jer 49:36 and Ezek 37:9. The passages in Daniel and Ezekiel are set in Babylonia. Zechariah speaks out of a community of Jews who have recently returned from Babylonia and is addressed to Jews who are still there. In Jer 49:36 the prophet addresses Elam when Judah is under Babylonian rule. The phrase 'the four winds (of heaven)' is not found in the Ugaritic texts but is quite common in Akkadian literature.

Enūma Eliš does not mention any of the kinds of animals in Dan 7 apart from lions. Also, it has no close parallels to their bizarre features. Nor can it explain the specific number and sequence of the beasts. Porter (1983) has argued that the animal imagery in Dan 7–8 has its background in Babylonian birth omens. These omens were based on the observation of any malformed or imperfect newborn creature, miscarriages as well as live births. They were collected in series for consultation. Lions, leopards and bears are found in these omens, and some of the features of the beasts in Dan 7–8 can be found in them, such as animals with one horn or two horns with one shorter than the other. Winged creatures are not mentioned. No exact parallels to Daniel's beasts can be found. Despite this, these omens do provide a credible background to Daniel's bizarre animal imagery. For readers unaware of these omens the imagery is simply bizarre, even absurd. However, for those aware of the strange animal forms recorded in birth omens the imagery would evoke a sense of the ominous and so compel attention. This suggests that it comes from a Jewish community embedded in Mesopotamian culture because this is the only culture in the ancient Near East, apart from the Hittites in Anatolia (*ca.* 1650–1200 BCE), in which such omens were important. In addition, in the light of the laws on clean and unclean animals, such hybrid creatures would be regarded as unclean, and so the beasts in Daniel would also act as symbols of evil.

When discussing the dream in Dan 2 the wide consensus that the four kingdoms in that dream and the vision of Dan 7 are: Babylon, Media, Persia and Macedon was noted. Some consider the inclusion of Media as odd because the Medes never ruled over Judea and the Babylonian Empire survived the Median Empire by just over a decade. Its inclusion may be explained as due to the author's imperfect knowledge of history, though some commentators argue that the imagery of the ram in Dan 8 indicates a reasonably accurate knowledge of the relationship of the Median and Persian Empires. Another explanation suggested is that the author has taken over and adapted an existing scheme without much regard to history. There is evidence of a traditional 'three-kingdom' sequence of Assyria, Media and Persia in the eastern Mediterranean (e.g. Herodotus, *Hist.* 1.95, 130). In *Sibylline Oracle* 4:49–101 the sequence is extended to Assyria, Media, Persia and Macedonia. This oracle probably dates from soon after the age of Alexander (*OTP* 1:381–389). A fragment of Aemilius Sura, of uncertain date, has the same sequence. This indicates that in the eastern Mediterranean world the Median Empire was seen as a distinct and important entity. This is because the Medes joined the Babylonians in destroying the Assyrian Empire and then annexed its northern and eastern portions. The Babylonian Empire was at the peak of its power under Nebuchadnezzar. After his death it was weakened by court intrigues and Media could be seen as the major power in the eastern Mediterranean world until Cyrus rebelled and brought the Persians to the fore (see CAH 2:110–48). So, from the perspective of an author in Babylonia, the sequence Babylon, Media, Persia and Macedonian would not show a disregard for history but reflect their own experience of who was 'top nation'. The objection that Media never ruled over Judea may be met by looking at history from the point of view of a Jewish exile in Babylonia. 2 Kgs 17:6; 18:11 state that when the Assyrians deported many Israelites, they settled some 'in the cities of the Medes'. Tobit's instruction to his son (Tob 14) also witnesses to the importance of Media to the eastern dispersion. While the Judeans were experiencing the rule of Babylon, their exiled kin were experiencing the rule of Media. The structure of the dream and vision requires that the empires be presented sequentially, but there is no reason why they should not overlap and, as we have seen, the sequence may represent the order in which they were 'top power' in the eastern Mediterranean. The Judeans were interested in the plight of their northern kindred. Several oracles of the Judean prophets express the hope that those living in exile will return and be reunited with Judah under a Davidic king (e.g. Mic 5; Jer 30–31; Ezek 17). The author of Dan 9 was aware of Jeremiah's prophecies of restoration (v. 2) and the prayer expresses the distress of Judah, the inhabitants of Jerusalem and 'all Israel, those that are near and those that are far away, in all the lands to which you have driven them' (v. 7).

Sibylline Oracle 3:388–400 is probably the earliest evidence we have of the interpretation of Dan 7. It is part of a collection of oracles against the nations which date from before the Battle of Actium (31 BCE) (*OTP* 1:354–61) and this oracle may be from much earlier than that. It identifies the fourth kingdom as the Macedonian Empire. However, since at least the time of Josephus (*Ant.* 10.10.4 [10.208–10]), there has been an influential tradition of interpretation that has identified the fourth kingdom as the Roman Empire. The author of 2 *Esdras/4 Ezra*, writing at about the same time as Josephus, makes it clear that this is a break with the then-accepted interpretation: 'The eagle you saw coming up from the sea is the fourth kingdom, which appeared in the vision of your brother Daniel. But it was not explained to him as I now explain to you' (12:11–12). The end of Seleucid rule led to the domination of Judea by the Roman Empire and not the coming of the kingdom of God as many had hoped and expected. This was compounded by the destruction of the Jerusalem Temple by the Romans in 70 CE which no doubt, led Jewish exegetes to change the identification of the fourth beast from the Macedonian Empire to the Roman Empire. Early Christian scholars adopted this interpretation because, in their view, Jesus inaugurated the kingdom of God in the time of the Roman Empire (e.g. Irenaeus, *Adv. Haer.* 26.1). With Rome as the fourth empire the sequence becomes: Babylon, Medo-Persia, Macedonia and Rome. A minority of commentators still defend this position (e.g. Young, 1972: 141–50).

Identifying the fourth kingdom as the Roman Empire faces a number of problems.

1 In the vision of the statue nothing is said of the fourth kingdom that suggests Rome. The statement about marriage alliances (2:43) fits with the prominence given to those between the Ptolemies and Seleucids in Dan 11.

2 Nothing said about the fourth beast points specifically to Rome. The repeated statement that it is 'different from all the others' (7:7, 19) makes sense with regard to the Macedonian Empire since Alexander the Great was the first non-oriental conqueror of the Near East.

3 Making Rome the fourth kingdom requires making a distinction between the little horns of ch. 7 and ch. 8. They do have some distinctive features. However, if both little horns are Antiochus IV these can be seen to produce complementary, not contradictory, portraits of him and his career (Lucas, 2002: 214–15).

4 If the fourth kingdom is the Macedonian Empire, each of the 'prophetic surveys of history' in chs 2, 7, 8, and 11 has the same end-point, the persecution of the Jews by Antiochus IV. If that kingdom is Rome the survey in ch. 8 has a different end-point from the others and it is difficult to explain this.

Daniel 7: The throne scene

Discussion of possible backgrounds to the imagery of the throne scene in Dan 7:9–14 has been closely linked with the figure of 'one like a human being' (v. 13). The Aramaic phrase is literally, 'one like a son of man' but 'son of man' is an idiomatic way of saying 'human being', In the first half of the twentieth century Iranian mythology about Gayomart, the Primordial Man, was widely viewed as a background for this figure (see Mowinckel, 1956: 420–37). The Primordial Man is not the first created man but a cosmological figure. In Iranian mythology the world is thought of as arising from him in various ways (e.g. by emanation or being built up from his body parts). He is also connected with eschatology because when the new world comes, he will return in some form. It was argued that this 'Anthropos mythology' (*anthrōpos* is the Greek word for 'man, human being') existed in various forms in the Hellenistic Near East.

Following a strong critique of this position by Colpe (1961) there has been a growing consensus against it. A major weakness in it is that the

Anthropos figure with which the 'son of man' was compared was an artificial construct drawn from the various forms of the myth. Also, the 'son of man' figure with which the scholars worked was also a composite figure drawn from various Jewish texts, including some which had a 'messiah figure' but did not explicitly use the phrase 'son of man'. With regard to Dan 7 in particular, the 'one like a human being' has no 'primordial role'. Moreover, the Anthropos myths do not provide any illumination of the connection between the throne scene and the vision of the beasts.

An influential paper by Emerton (1958) drew attention to possible parallels between the Canaanite texts from Ugarit and Dan 7. Among these are a number which feature the god Baal. Emerton pointed out that in the Hebrew Bible clouds are associated with theophanies of YHWH. In Dan 7:13, however, the figure who comes with the clouds is clearly subordinate to the Ancient of Days. This combination of imagery is unprecedented in the Hebrew Bible but does fit with Canaanite mythology. In this Baal is subordinate to El and a stock epithet for Baal is 'rider/charioteer of the clouds'. El is portrayed as an aged person with a grey beard. One of the epithets used of him is *ʾab šnm*, which is usually translated as 'father of years'. Baal's battle with Yam/Sea for kingship and defeat of the monster *ltn*, discussed above, provides a link between the throne scene and the vision of the beasts. In response to this it has been pointed out that in Dan 7:13 the one like a human being comes *with* the clouds, not *riding on* them. The usual translation of El's epithet is disputed because the normal plural of 'years' in Ugaritic is *šnt*. The long time-gap between the Ugaritic texts (fourteenth/thirteenth century BCE) and the composition of Daniel has also been seen as problematic.

Mosca (1986) argues that Ps 89 provides a link between the Canaanite mythology and Dan 7. In this psalm YHWH sits 'in the council of the holy ones' (v. 7 [MT 8]). He rules the raging sea and has crushed Rahab (v. 9–10 [MT10–11]). His throne is mentioned (v. 14 [MT 15]). As the ultimate King of Israel, he gives kingship (v. 19 [MT 20]) and everlasting rule (v. 29 [30]) to the Davidic King. Goldingay (2019: 341–2) suggests that Ps 2 provides a significant background to the throne scene in Dan 7. In it the nations and kings conspire against YHWH and his anointed ruler. YHWH rebukes them and affirms that his anointed 'son' will crush them and rule over them. These psalms reflect the Judean theology of kingship, which probably took over royal rites and imagery from the Canaanite practices in Jerusalem when David made it his capital. These were used to express the distinctive understanding of the covenant between YHWH and the Davidic dynasty of kings. The phrase 'son of man' occurs in Ps 8:4b [MT 8:5b]. In Hebrew, as in Aramaic, it means 'human being', Here it expresses the unimpressiveness and insignificance of humans compared to God. Significantly, the following verses of Ps 8 parallels what is said in Gen 1:26–28 about God giving dominion over the non-human creatures to humans. This understanding of the role of humans could provide a conceptual link between the two visions in Dan 7. The dominion that was exercised by the beasts is given to one like a human being.

Another passage in the Hebrew Bible that has similarities to Dan 7 is the description of YHWH's chariot throne in Ezek 1. There is a stormy wind and four animal creatures, each with four faces and four wings. In the middle of these are burning coals of fire and above them a throne with more fire and a human-like figure. In Ezekiel the prophet is often addressed as 'son of man'. This seems to emphasize his humanness, and perhaps weakness, in contrast to the deity.

On balance it seems likely that some of the imagery in the throne scene has its origin in Canaanite mythology but that it has been mediated to the author through the Hebrew biblical traditions. This is particularly the case with regard to the Judean ideology of kingship which was celebrated in the temple cult in Jerusalem.

Daniel 7: The 'One Like a Human Being' and 'the Holy Ones of the Most High'

Unlike the beasts, who are destroyed or stripped of their dominion, the 'one like a human being' is given 'dominion and glory, and kingship'. Daniel 7:13–14 clearly describes an investiture. The phrase 'peoples, nations and languages' has been used earlier in Daniel to describe the rule claimed by Nebuchadnezzar (3:4, 7, 29; 4:1 [MT 3:31]; 5:19) and Darius (6:25). Only God's rule, however, is described as everlasting (2:44; 4:3 [MT 3:33]; 4:34 [MT 31]; 6:26). This forms a parallel with the end of the dream in Dan 2. It is equivalent to the stone 'cut out, not by human hands' destroying the statue and becoming a great mountain that filled the earth. What is being symbolized in both cases is the establishment of God's rule in a new and direct form.

Some scholars, however (see Collins, 1993: 305) argue that the 'Ancient of Days' is a different kind of symbol from the beasts, being mythic-realistic rather than allegorical. They then argue that the same must be true of 'the one like a human being'. This is usually combined with a tendency to treat vv. 9–10 as a quite separate vision from that in vv. 2–8. It seems more natural, however, to take it as 'scene 2' of the same vision, and there seems no reason why a vision should not move between different kinds of symbol, just as story moves between different kinds of characters. The appearance and investiture of the 'one like a human being' is the climax of the whole vision and the implied contrast with the beasts and their fate favours the view that it is the same kind of symbol. Just as they represent kingdoms, in their case earthly ones, so this figure represents a kingdom, God's kingdom. Perhaps this is the significance of the cloud imagery with its association with theophany. Most scholars, however, have not been prepared to accept the figure of the 'one like a human being' as simply part of a symbol of the establishing of God's rule. They have debated whether the figure is a corporate or individual one and whether it is an angel or a human being. This has been closely tied up with the debate about the identity of 'the holy ones of the Most High' and it is helpful to discuss that first.

In the Hebrew Bible the phrase 'the holy ones of the Most High' occurs only in Dan 7:18, 22, 25 and 27. In the Hebrew Bible the word qᵊdôšîm (equivalent to the Aramaic qaddîšîn), a plural adjective used as a noun, 'holy ones', usually refers to heavenly beings. The only undisputed use of it referring to human beings is Ps 34:9 [MT 10], with its use in Deut 33:2 and Ps 16:3 being debatable cases. In Daniel, outside ch. 7, 'holy ones' on its own occurs in Aramaic in 4:13, 17, 23 [MT 10, 14, 20] and in Hebrew in 8:13. In all these cases it refers to heavenly beings. This semantic evidence leads some (e.g. Collins, 1993, 312–18) to understand the holy ones of the Most High as angels. Others, however (e.g. Hartman and Di Lella, 1978: 89–102), reject this view.

1   They argue that although use of 'holy one(s)' to refer to human beings is rare, it is not unprecedented outside Daniel in both the Hebrew Bible and non-biblical Jewish literature. What it refers to in Dan 7 must be decided on the context in that chapter.

2   In view of the past tense used, what is said about the small horn's actions against the 'holy ones' in 7:21, 25 fits most naturally with Antiochus' actions against faithful Jews. It is hard to see how he could wage war against angels. In response to this it is pointed out that in 8:10 the little horn cast down 'some of the host and some of the stars, and trampled on them', indicating a transcendent aspect to its actions.

3 Most scholars take 'the people of the holy ones of the Most High' who are given kingship and dominion in 7:27 as referring to the Jewish people. This is taken as fundamental to the interpretation of 7:13–14 and as implying that the shorter phrase in 7:18, 22 also refers to the Jews. It is, however, pointed out that while the phrase in 7:27 can be taken to mean, 'the people which consists of the holy ones of the Most High', it could alternatively be taken as meaning, 'the people who belong to the holy ones of the Most High' and so maintain a distinction between the human people, the Jews, and the angelic host.

4 It is also argued that the 'angelic interpretation' results in the vision giving little encouragement to the faithful Jews who are facing persecution. To this it is replied that chs 10–12 show that there is a transcendent dimension to the conflict and that victory in the heavenly battle means victory for the Jews on Earth.

This last point suggests a possible resolution to this debate. Maybe our modern world view leads commentators to be prone to make a strong dichotomy between heaven/earth and angel/human which the author(s) and readers of Daniel would not share. They may therefore be looking for an unambiguous solution to the terminology when the original readers would not be worried by ambiguity (cf. Goldingay, 2019: 377). Daniel 10–12 does present a world view in which things and events on Earth have a heavenly counterpart. In 7:18, 22 the ambiguous term 'the holy ones of the Most High' may be used deliberately to reflect the fact that earthly events have a heavenly aspect. The phrase 'the people of the holy ones of the Most High' in 7:27 most probably does refer to the persecuted Jews and is used to assure them that they will share in the everlasting kingdom.

Scholars who have adopted an angelic interpretation of 'the holy ones of the Most High' have sometimes adopted an individualistic, angelic, interpretation of the 'one like a human being'. Daniel is the only book in the Hebrew Bible which gives names to angels, and the angelic figures in Dan 10–12 are presented as having a human form. The two angels that are named are Gabriel and Michael. Each has been identified with the 'one like a human being' but Michael is the more likely candidate since he is described to Daniel as 'your prince' (10:21) and as 'the protector of your people' (12:1) (Collins, 1993: 310; Newsom, 2014: 236).

Individualistic, human, interpretations of the 'one like a human being' have very occasionally proposed an identification with Judas Maccabeus.

This, however, is unlikely because, as we will see in ch. 4, nowhere else in Daniel is any clear support given to the military action of the Maccabees and most commentators take Dan 11:34 as a dismissive reference to it. Much more common has been the identification of this figure with an individual, messianic, figure. However, only a minority of recent scholars have supported this view (e.g. Beasley-Murray, 1983). This is because Daniel, seems to lack any messianic hope in the strict sense of expecting a future kingly deliverer from the line of David. There are two references to 'an anointed one' in Dan 9:25–26 (not '*the* anointed one' as in some English translations). The first of these is called 'an anointed prince' and seems to be a separate person from the second one. Nothing suggests that either of them is the Davidic Messiah of later Judaism. Possible identifications of them have been discussed above in Excursus 1 in ch. 2.

Since the nineteenth century a corporate interpretation of 'the one like a human being' has found many supporters (e.g. Hartman and Di Lella, 1978: 85–102). This equates the figure with 'the people of the holy ones of the Most High' and 'the holy ones of the Most High', both understood as the faithful, persecuted, Jews. In Ps 80:17 [MT 80:18] the phrase 'son of man' stands in parallel with 'the man of your right hand': 'But let your hand be upon the man at your right hand, the son of man whom you made strong for yourself' (literal translation). The 'man at your right hand' seems to refer to Israel, perhaps represented by the Davidic King. This indicates the 'son of man' could be used in a collective sense.

Daniel 8:23–25 and 11:3–45

The long survey of history in Dan 11:3–45, composed of fairly short, enigmatically phrased sentences about apparently future events, has no analogy elsewhere in the Hebrew Bible, except in Dan 8:23–25. From the early twentieth century onwards scholars studying Akkadian texts occasionally commented on the similarity of a few of these to the passages in Daniel. A paper by Grayson and Lambert (1964) bringing together the known texts and adding new material stimulated new interest in these texts by Akkadian scholars and also by scholars interested in apocalyptic literature, including Daniel. This led to the uncovering of new texts belonging to this group and new copies or further fragments of the known texts. There are now five 'core' texts: the Marduk Prophecy, the Šulgi Prophecy, the Dynastic Prophecy, the Uruk Prophecy and a text labelled simply Text A. At least two other texts,

Text B and LBAT 1543, are similar to this group. All five texts are purported prophecies that take the form of concise, enigmatic, surveys of a series of rulers' reigns. The rulers are unnamed but referred to as 'a king/prince' or as 'the king of X'. In most cases, reasonable correlations have been proposed between the rulers and events alluded to in the texts and known historical rulers and events. If the texts originate from not long after the latest event they record, they come from various dates ranging from the twelfth (the Marduk Prophecy) to the third (the Dynastic Prophecy) centuries BCE (see Lucas, 2002: 269–70 for English translations of portions of the Uruk and Dynastic Prophecies). Grayson and Lambert called these texts 'Akkadian Prophecies' and others have called them 'Akkadian Apocalypses'. The appropriateness of both designations has been questioned.

There are some significant similarities between these texts and the passages in Daniel.

1 There is a similarity of *style*. Both sets of texts can be described as presenting a concise, enigmatic, survey of history with names replaced by ciphers and the verbs in the future tense.

2 There is a *semantic* similarity in the phrase often used in the Akkadian texts as a section divider '(after him) a king shall arise'. The Daniel passages do not have a regular section divider but do use a phrase similar to the Akkadian one (8:25; 11:2, 3, 7, 20, 21; 12:1). The Akkadian texts use the verb *elû* for 'arise' in the sense of 'appear, come on the scene'. In Daniel the verb used is *'āmad*, which in the Hebrew of the later biblical books is the required sematic equivalent rather than the strict cognate of the Akkadian verb, *'ālāh*. The phrase 'after him' is *arkišu* (a preposition with a personal suffix) in Akkadian. There is no Hebrew preposition cognate to *arki*. In Dan 11:7, 20, 21, *('al) kannô* (in his place) has the equivalent meaning. The Akkadian texts use both *šarru* and *rubû* to refer to the rulers. The Hebrew equivalent of both these words when referring to a ruler is *melek*. The strict cognates would not convey the correct meaning.

3 A third similarity is in the command to *secrecy* in Dan 8:26 ('seal up the vision') and 12:4 ('keep the words secret and the book sealed') and the 'secrecy colophon' of the Dynastic Prophecy in which the reader is charged not to show it to 'the uninitiated'.

Lambert (1978: 15) gave an additional reason for suggesting a direct link between the passages in Daniel and the Akkadian Prophecies. This is the lack of comparable material from elsewhere, including Egyptian and Greek literature pre-dating Daniel. He presumed that the whole of Daniel originated in Judea, which he recognized raised a problem. How could a Jew in Palestine know of the Akkadian Prophecies? First, there is the problem of the difficult cuneiform script. Then there is the fact that, by the Seleucid era the Akkadian language was the preserve of the scholarly community, having been replaced in common use by Aramaic. Finally, that only a handful of these texts exist suggests that they represent an esoteric, though long-standing, branch of Akkadian literature. This is supported by the fact that they use phraseology that has close similarities to that used in astrological omens, another esoteric branch of Akkadian literature. Lambert suggested that the Akkadian Prophecies must have been translated into Aramaic or Greek, but admitted that there was no evidence for this. If they had been available in either of these languages one might expect writers other than the author(s) of Daniel would have been influenced by them. A survey of a wide range of Jewish and Christian works that might be expected to show such influence found no evidence of this (Lucas, 2002: 271–2). This strongly suggests that Dan 8:23–25 and 11:3–45 were composed by an author, or authors, among the exiles in Babylonia, skilled in the language and literature of the Chaldeans, including the omen literature, as the story in Dan 1 indicates.

Conclusion

This survey of the imagery in the dreams and visions in Daniel shows that it has a variety of sources alongside the material taken from Hebrew traditions now found in the Hebrew Bible. Particularly striking is the evidence from the vision in ch. 7 and the surveys of history in chs 8:23–25 and 12:3–45 that the author(s) were immersed in Babylonian cultural imagery and probably acquainted with esoteric Akkadian literature. Such a person would be the kind of wise man that is depicted in the stories in Daniel. The knowledge of wider, Hellenistic, imagery displayed in the dream in ch. 2 might also be expected in someone in this position. Also, the sequence of kingdoms in the dream of ch. 2 and the vision of ch. 7 makes best sense if it reflects the world view of a Jew living in the Babylonian Dispersion rather than in Judea.

4

Daniel: Resisting pressure

Investigations

1 In what ways do the stories in Dan 1–6 present the rule of Gentile kings positively, and in what ways negatively? Where do you think the balance lies?

2 Within the survey of history in Dan 11:2–45, the careers of four kings stand out: the 'warrior king' (vv. 3–4); the 'king of the north' of vv. 10–19; the king of v. 20; the 'contemptible person' (vv. 21–45). Because of the amount of space given to him, the last person is the focus of the survey. How are some aspects of his career foreshadowed by those of the earlier kings? What do you think is the significance of this?

Daniel 1–6: The pressure of exile

Daniel 1

Anyone living as an exile or immigrant in a foreign culture will feel under pressure to conform to that culture. The spectrum of possible responses to this pressure runs from assimilation to the new culture, which certainly removes the pressure, to withdrawing into an enclave of one's own culture so as to avoid contact with the foreign culture as far as possible, which will relieve the pressure to some extent. The opening story in Daniel presents this issue of how to respond to the pressure to conform to a foreign culture.

On the face of it, Nebuchadnezzar's command concerning some of the young noblemen among the Judean captives brought to Babylon is a generous one. They will be given three years of education to fit them to serve as courtiers in the king's palace, during which they would be given a daily allocation of food from the royal rations. Of course, from the king's perspective it was making use of a potentially valuable resource that was part of his war booty – the skills and gifts of these young men. Daniel and his three friends, however, do not welcome this opportunity without hesitation: 'Daniel resolved that he would not defile himself with the royal rations of food and wine' (v. 8). There have been various suggestions as to what lies behind this reaction. The most likely ones are:

1 The mention of 'defilement' suggests, to many, that the Mosaic food laws lie behind Daniel's decision. In other places the Hebrew verb used for this here (*gāʾal*) refers to ritual defilement (Ezra 2:62; Neh 7:64; Lam 4:14; Mal 1:7, 12). The palace caterers would not follow the Mosaic laws about which animals could be eaten and how they were to be killed. This concern would not include vegetables, which Daniel is happy to accept (v. 12). But the Mosaic laws say nothing about wine, except in the special case of the Nazarite vow (Num 6: 2–4). So, concern about the Mosaic food laws is only a partial reason for Daniel's decision.

2 Some suggest that the issue was avoidance of idolatry. Daniel may have been concerned that the food had come from the temple and had been offered to a pagan deity. This, however, could also have been true of the vegetarian food which he was willing to eat. In fact, as far as food specifically offered to the deity was concerned, only the king and perhaps a few senior temple officials were allowed to eat it (Oppenheim, 1977, 189). Also, in the exilic and post-exilic writings in the Hebrew Bible, mention of idols and idolatry usually has a strong polemical tone. It would be surprising to have merely an implicit reference to it here.

3 Others think that it is significant that it is the *king's* food that Daniel rejects (vv. 5, 8). The word used for this, פַּתְבַּג (*patbag*), is a rare one and its use in Dan 11:25b–26a is seen as a clue to its importance. Here it is clear that plots against the king by those who have eaten such 'royal rations' are considered unexpected and particularly reprehensible. This suggests that to accept and eat such food was to commit oneself

to loyal allegiance to the king. To this might be added the significance of meals in general in the ancient Near East. This is indicated by their connection with covenant-making (e.g. Gen 31:44–54; Exod 24:1–11). All this, however, does not explain the use of the term 'defile'.

Of course, Daniel's decision may have been prompted by more than one factor. Drawing on anthropological studies, Fewell (1991:17–18) notes that there is a close parallel between the programme set out for the Judean exiles by Nebuchadnezzar (vv. 3–7, 18–19) and the classic model of a 'rite of passage', a ritual intended to mark and enable a person's moving from one phase of life to another. This has three basic stages: the person is separated from their community and put in seclusion; while secluded they are fed special food and taught special knowledge, with the aim of establishing new allegiances and a new identity; the person is then reintegrated into society. We have noted in Chapter 3 that the scribal training implied by being 'taught the literature and language of the Chaldeans' (v. 4) was a means of induction into the culture, way of thought and religion of Babylon. Seen in this context, the renaming of Daniel and his companions takes on a special significance. Renaming was a common way of indicating new ownership and new allegiance (e.g. 2 Kgs 23:34; 24:17). In this case names that express attributes of the God of Israel are replaced by names which probably invoke Babylonian deities. Daniel means, 'God is my judge' or 'God has judged'. Hananiah and Azariah both use an abbreviated form of the divine name YHWH, 'Yah'. They mean, respectively, 'Yah has been Gracious' and 'Yah has helped'. Mishael expresses the incomparability of Israel's God, 'Who is what God is?' The meaning of the Babylonian names is unclear. Daniel 4:8 links the name Belteshazzar with 'Bel', a title for Marduk, the patron deity of Babylon. It may mean, '(Bel) guard his life' or 'Lady protect the king' (addressing Bel's consort). Abednego may be a (deliberately?) corrupt translation into Hebrew of an Akkadian name meaning 'servant of Nabu'. It is possible that all the names in the MT are deliberately corrupted forms of names extolling Babylonian deities (Pace, 2008: 33). The Judean exiles are being put under pressure to change their allegiance to the Babylonian king and his gods, and to adopt a Babylonian way of life. They are to move from being faithful Jews to being loyal Babylonians.

Fewell (1991: 20) argues that in the dialogue between Daniel and palace officials in vv. 10–13 the narrator indicates that there is a possible political aspect to Daniel's decision. She points out that the palace master's words in

v. 10 can be read in two ways, depending on the meaning given to the phrase *pənêkem zōʿăpîm*. The phrase is normally taken to refer to a poor physical condition because the first word ('your faces') can refer to physical appearances and the second word can mean 'out of sorts'. However, the first word can be taken to refer to a person's attitude and the second word can mean 'displeased, angry' so that the sense is an attitude of dissent, even defiance, towards the king. So, refusing to eat the royal portion could be seen as an act of political dissent. This would increase the danger of the courtier losing his head if he agreed to Daniel's request. Despite this setback, Daniel does not give up. Using tact and diplomacy Daniel approaches the minor official put in personal charge of himself and his friends with the proposal of a short test of an alternative diet. In his speech in v. 13 he uses a word for 'appearance' (*marʾēh*) that refers unambiguously to someone's physical appearance. The narrator makes it clear (vv. 9, 17) that Daniel's success in being granted the test and its positive outcome was the result of God blessing him and his companions.

Faced with pressure to become a loyal Babylonian Daniel does not respond either by accepting assimilation into Babylonian culture or by withdrawing from it. In his situation the latter would mean refusing to take part in Nebuchadnezzar's training programme, which would doubtless have meant losing his head. Some might have accepted that as necessary martyrdom. Daniel, however, opted for 'critical engagement' with Babylonian culture. Learning about a culture, including its religion, does not require assimilating to it, but can be a basis for critical involvement in it. Accepting a position in the royal court will involve hard choices, but might give the opportunity for influencing affairs in positive ways. If such critical engagement is to be possible Daniel and his friends need to retain their identity and integrity as faithful Jews. In Daniel's view this means drawing lines to maintain their distinctiveness. Exactly where that line was drawn may not have mattered greatly, but his choice may well have been influenced by the Mosaic food laws. In this case the stand to resist the pressure of the Babylon court culture was made tactfully and privately.

This opening story encourages the Judean exiles to adopt the approach portrayed by Daniel and his companions. They are not to hold back from involvement in the surrounding pagan culture but to maintain their distinctive faith while getting involved in it. It assures them that their God will bless them in this endeavour. The story holds out the possibility that they may even achieve positions of influence in that society.

Daniel 2

This story presents another way in which critical involvement in an alien society can lead to problems. In it, Daniel and his companions face the risk of death, not because of their ethnicity or religion, but because they have been willing to be counted among the sages of Babylon.

The Hebrew in Nebuchadnezzar's speech in v. 3 is ambiguous. A literalistic translation is, 'my spirit is troubled to know the dream'. This could mean, as Josephus infers (*Ant.* 10.10.3 [10.195]), that the king has forgotten the dream. However, that would make the test set in v. 9 a bluff, since it would be meaningless unless the king remembered enough of the dream to be able to be sure that he would recognize the account of it offered by the Chaldeans. It is therefore reasonable to take 'know' here in the sense of, 'perceive the meaning of, understand'. His testing of the sages has parallels in the ancient Near East. Sennacherib separated the diviners into groups on at least one occasion to reduce collusion between them, in order to test the reliability of their answer (Oppenheim, 1977: 227). According to Herodotus (*Hist.* 1.47), Croesus tested oracles, including the renowned ones of Delphi and Ammon, in order to find out which could be trusted to give a reliable answer to his question whether or not to invade Persia.

The Chaldean's response that no human sage could do what the king asked because to do so required a revelation from the gods, 'whose dwelling is not with mortals' (vv. 10–11) sets the scene for Daniel. He and his companions pray for just such a revelation. When it is granted and Daniel goes to give it to the king, he prefaces it by echoing the words of the Chaldeans and asserting that he can tell Nebuchadnezzar the dream and its interpretation, not because of his own wisdom, but because 'there is a God in heaven who reveals mysteries' and has chosen to give this revelation to Nebuchadnezzar (vv. 27–30). After Daniel has described the dream and given its interpretation the king falls on his face and worships Daniel saying, 'Truly, your God is God of gods and Lord of kings and a revealer of mysteries' (v. 46). Both Jewish and Christian commentators have been embarrassed by Daniel's apparent acceptance of this worship. Neither the author of Daniel nor Josephus (*Ant.* 10.10.5 [10.211–12]) saw any problem here. Perhaps for them the important thing was the symbolism of a pagan king prostrate before a representative of the God of Israel (cf. Isa 45:14; 49:23; 60:14).

For the original hearers and readers, the encouraging message of the story is that they will be given the ability to cope with the problems of living as faithful Jews under the pressures of exile. Indeed, these problems may provide opportunities to witness to the greatness of their God. The importance of the story is not just that God gave Daniel the revelation he needed, but also in what it says about God. The theological message is summed up in Daniel's expression of praise to the God of his ancestors (vv. 20–23) which asserts that 'he knows what is in the darkness, and light dwells in him' (which is why he could reveal the dream and its interpretation to Daniel) and that 'He changes times and seasons, deposes kings and sets up kings' (which is the message of the dream). So, the exiles can take courage because nothing is hidden from their God, who knows what is happening to them, and is ultimately in control of events.

Daniel 3

In chapter 1 Daniel and his friends were able to draw a line and disobey Nebuchadnezzar's command in a discreet way without any adverse public reaction. In this story Shadrach, Meshach and Abednego are forced into a public confrontation with the king.

Commentators debate the nature of the statue set up by Nebuchadnezzar, where it was placed, and the purpose of the event described. What is clear is that Daniel's companions decided that their critical engagement with Babylonian culture required them to draw a line about involvement in the event. As in ch. 1, the line seems based on the Mosaic law, in this case the first two commandments of the Decalogue (v. 18). Down through the centuries these presented Diaspora Jews who wanted to be involved with the social and political life of a foreign city with a dilemma. In the late first century CE, Apion asked the question, 'If the Jews be citizens of Alexandria, why do they not worship the same gods as the Alexandrians?' (Josephus, *Contra Ap.* 2.6 [2.65]). The Chaldeans who denounced Shadrach, Meshach and Abednego seem to have been motivated more by professional envy than religion (v. 12). That envy, though, was heightened by xenophobia.

The only time that Shadrach, Meshach and Abednego speak in Daniel is in vv. 16–18, but the import of what they say is a subject of debate because of problems in translating v. 17. Coxon (1976) gives many examples of how the perceived theological problem of this verse has strongly influenced both translations and interpretations of the verse. The theological problem is that the three exiles express doubt about either their God's power or his existence. The linguistic problem is how to interpret the opening words, אִיתַי הֵן (hēn 'ītay). In Aramaic hēn means 'if' and introduces a conditional sentence, 'ītay means 'there is/are'. All the ancient versions, presumably for theological reasons, ignore the conditionality of the sentence. The LXX makes it a creedal statement, 'For there is a God in heaven, our one Lord whom we fear, who is able to deliver us ...'. The Vg treats the *hēn* as if it were the Hebrew word *hinnēh*, 'behold' (a sense that *hēn* does not have in Aramaic) and reads, 'For behold, our God, whom we worship, is able to rescue us ...'. The opening words clearly mean, 'If there is/exists ...'. The question is how they should be taken. There are three possibilities.

1 They can be taken on their own: 'If it be so ...'
2 They can be taken with the next word: 'If our God exists...'
3 They can be taken with the following participle: 'If our God is able ...'

The first possibility is favoured by the older English versions, 'If it be so, our God whom we serve is able to deliver us from the burning fiery furnace and he will deliver us out of thine hand, O king' (King James Version, cf. Revised Version, Revised Standard Version). This is the least likely option because the opening words then have to refer back to the king's threat ('If it is carried out ... '). This, however, leaves the corresponding condition at the start of v. 18 ('If not ... ') without any natural reference point. The New International Version (2011) main text deals with this problem by a rather forced paraphrasing of vv. 17–18, adding words not in the MT: 'If we are thrown into the blazing furnace, the God whom we serve is able to deliver us from it, and he will deliver us from Your Majesty's hand. But even if he does not, we want you to know ... ' Both of the other two possibilities rest on a more natural reading of the two conditional sentences as balancing one another. The second possibility is less likely of the two because the king has not questioned the existence of the God of the Jews, but the ability of any god to save the Jews from the furnace. The Revised English Bible adopts it, but only by means of an interpretive paraphrase: 'If there is a god who is able to save us from the blazing furnace, it is our God whom we serve; he will deliver us from your majesty's power'. The alternative marginal readings of these versions and the main text of some newer English versions (e.g. Jerusalem Bible, New Revised Standard Version) have taken up the third possibility, 'If our God whom we serve is able to deliver us ... let him deliver us. But if not ...'. There is a grammatical objection to this interpretation. The use of the particle *'itay* with a participle is well established as an idiom in Aramaic, but in its other uses in biblical Aramaic nothing is placed between the particle and the participle. However, Coxon gives a few examples in non-biblical Aramaic where words do intervene. He argues that in Dan 3:17 the desire to give prominence to 'our God' as the subject explains the unusual word order. He also argues for influence from a parallel construction in Akkadian, in which the corresponding particle can be separated from its governing verb.

Among commentators who accept the third possibility as the most likely grammatically some seek to soften the apparent expression of doubt in the ability of the God of Israel to deliver the Jews from the furnace. One suggestion is that the uncertainty is not about God's omnipotence but his 'sovereign good pleasure'. Would their deliverance be in accordance with his holy and righteous will? This seems an over-subtle reading between the lines. Another is that the Jews accept the possibility of their God's inability to deliver them only 'for the sake of argument'. This, too, goes against the obvious meaning of the text without good grounds for doing so. Others argue that to deny that the story could be depicting any real doubt about God's ability to deliver these Jews is to make it unrealistic. As Collins (1993:188) says, 'Any Jew of the post-exilic period must have known that God, for whatever reason, does not always deliver the faithful'. For some, this must have raised the question of God's ability to do so. That this was the case for some Judean exiles in Babylon is shown by Isa 50:2 in which YHWH asks, 'Is my hand shortened, that it cannot redeem? Or have I no power to deliver?' These questions, and the oracle that contains them, only makes sense as a response to exiles who were denying, or doubting, YHWH's ability to deliver them.

Whatever their interpretation of v. 17, most commentators agree that the point being made in v. 18 is that the Jews' primary reason for not giving way to the king's demand is not their confidence that God will deliver them, but their adherence to the commandments of the Decalogue. Their stand is one of principle and not of prudence. The implication is that they are committed to their God not because of his power but because of the pattern of life that this commitment involves. They are concerned about morality not might.

A key feature in the denouement of the story is that Shadrach, Meshach and Abednego were not just saved *from* the furnace by miraculous fiat but were kept safe *in* the furnace by the presence of a fourth figure, with the 'appearance of a son of the gods' (v. 25) until Nebuchadnezzar calls them out of it. The original hearers and readers would very probably have seen a metaphorical meaning in this. The captivity in Egypt is compared to an 'iron furnace/smelter' in the Deuteronomic traditions (Deut 4:20; 1 Kgs 8:51; Jer 11:4). The experience of the exile in Babylon is described as the 'furnace of adversity' (Isa 48:10). The story would therefore resonate with those experiencing the pressures of exile in Babylon and assure them that they could know the presence of their God with them, as promised by the prophet, 'when you walk through the fire you shall not be burned, and the flame shall not consume you' (Isa 43:2). This would encourage them to emulate Shadrach, Meshach and Abednego's stand for what was right in principle, whatever the outcome might be. In his response to their deliverance Nebuchadnezzar recognizes that, 'they disobeyed the king's command and yielded up their bodies rather than serve and worship any god except their own God' (3:28) They have demonstrated the sovereignty of God over the king and set an example of open, passive, resistance to human sovereignty when it challenges God's sovereignty.

Daniel 4 and 5

In both these stories Daniel has to convey a message of judgement to a king. Speaking truth to those in power, including words of judgement to a king, was a function of prophets in Israel and Judah. For any courtier that is a difficult task, but especially so when the courtier is a foreigner from a conquered nation. In these stories of 'court contest' this task falls to Daniel because of the inability of the other sages to interpret the divine message that the king receives. The tone of the two stories is very different.

In Dan 4 Nebuchadnezzar has a frightening dream. He probably senses that it presages bad news. He sees a great and strong tree with beautiful foliage and abundant fruit. It provides food and shelter for all creatures. At the command of a heavenly being it is cut down leaving only a stump, which is bound with a band of iron and bronze. The tree is then seen to be a cipher for some person because the heavenly being says that 'he' (not 'it') is to live with the animals of the field and his mind to be changed from that of a human to that of an animal for 'seven times'. This is to happen so that 'all who live may know that the Most High is sovereign over the kingdom of mortals; he gives it to whom he will' (v. 17).

On hearing Nebuchadnezzar's account of the dream Daniel is visibly distressed and terrified. The reader is not told whether this is because he fears the consequences of being the bringer of bad news or because he likes the king and is genuinely sorry about what is about to happen to him. When the king encourages him to speak, Daniel's first words, 'My Lord, may the dream be for those who hate you, and its interpretation for your enemies!' show that what he is about to tell the king is something that he himself does not wish to happen. Does this express his true feelings for the king or is it just a diplomatic way of preparing him for bad news? Daniel's interpretation confirms that the dream is a decree of judgement on Nebuchadnezzar, though there is a message of hope in the preservation of the stump and the promise of restoration after 'seven times' have passed. He ends with a word of counsel to the king, 'atone for your sins with righteousness, and your iniquities with mercy to the oppressed, so that your prosperity may be prolonged' (v. 27). This does not specify what 'sins' and 'iniquities' the king has committed. This counsel seems to offer a postponement of judgement rather than its revocation in response to a change of behaviour by the king. Lacocque (1979: 81), however, argues that it is not clear that this 'decree' is different in kind from the pronouncements of judgement by Hebrew prophets which seem to be final, but can be revoked in response to genuine repentance (e.g. Jonah at Nineveh). In Mesopotamia it was assumed that evil omens were warnings of what would happen and that, if the warnings were heeded and the right actions taken, the evil could be averted. Oppenheim (1977: 222) notes that the series of dream omens began and ended with conjurations and the pertinent rituals for warding off the consequences of dreams predicting disasters or other ills. What Daniel counsels here is not some ritual but a change in moral behaviour.

The final part of the story indicates that the essence of Nebuchadnezzar's sin is pride. The judgement falls as he utters an egotistical speech about the magnificence of Babylon which he had built for his own glory. This speech would remind the original hearers and readers of the story of the Tower of Babel (Gen 11:1–9). After his restoration he extols the King of heaven 'for all his works are truth, and his ways justice; and he is able to bring low those who walk in pride'. Collins (1993: 234) sums up the message of this story as expressing 'a stubborn hope for the reclamation of even the most arrogant tyrant and for universal recognition of the Most High God'. This hope might encourage the exiles to persevere in their critical engagement with Babylonian society.

Daniel 5 is intended to be read in conjunction with Daniel 4. The stories in these two chapters, about the humbling of royal hubris, are the centre of the chiastic group formed by Dan 2–7 (see ch. 1). The references to Nebuchadnezzar in v. 2 and then v. 11 prepare the way for the comparison and contrast between Belshazzar and his 'father' made by Daniel in vv. 18–23. The issue of Belshazzar's relationship to Nebuchadnezzar will be discussed in ch. 5. Whatever one decides about that, within the context of the stories in Dan 1–6 the use of father–son language, rather than referring to

Nebuchadnezzar as simply a predecessor as king, can be understood as a way of enhancing the contrast between Nebuchadnezzar and Belshazzar.

No reason is given for Belshazzar holding his great feast. Nebuchadnezzar's arrogance arose from his great achievements. He could boast of Babylon 'which I built' and of 'my mighty power' and 'my glorious majesty' (Dan 4:30). Fewell (1991: 81–6) argues that Belshazzar's arrogant actions arose from his insecurity due to a lack of achievements. He held the feast in an attempt to win the allegiance of his subjects and to consolidate his political power. In chs 2 and 3 Nebuchadnezzar could command the obedience of his officials with threats of death. Belshazzar can only cajole his officials with food and wine. Under the influence of wine, he sends for the temple vessels which Nebuchadnezzar had brought from Jerusalem to Babylon (Dan 1:1–2). These symbolize one of Nebuchadnezzar's achievements. By using them as he does, he 'goes one better' than his 'father' by doing something that he might claim was more courageous. Nebuchadnezzar recognized the vessels as sacred and put them in the temple of his god. Belshazzar is ready to make profane use of them and also to use them to make libations to other gods. He has no respect for, and is not afraid of, the god to whom they were originally dedicated!

The response to Belshazzar's arrogant blasphemy is as swift as it was to Nebuchadnezzar's arrogant boasting. He is terrified by seeing a hand writing on the plaster of the wall. He cries out for all his wise men but when they arrive 'they could not read the writing or tell the king the interpretation' (v. 8). The 'queen' who comes in unbidden and has a longer memory than Belshazzar is probably the queen mother, who was often an important political figure in ancient Near Eastern courts. She extols the powers of Daniel which led Nebuchadnezzar to make him chief of all the sages and recommends that he be sent for.

Writing from a feminist perspective Athalya Brenner (2001: 238–9) sees the presentation of Belshazzar as an example of the 'obtuse foreign male ruler trope' in the Hebrew Bible. This uses bitter satire to belittle the ruler whose ineptitude is emphasized by a contrasting image of a woman who is smarter and more competent than he is. Brenner sees the feast as having orgiastic elements. She argues that the Aramaic phrase 'and the knots of his loins became loose' (v. 6, NRSV: 'His limbs gave way') is crude humour implying sexual impotence and loss of bowel control. Belshazzar is 'demoted at once from sexual adult male to an asexual child who cannot control his bowel and/or bladder movements'. His male advisors cannot help him. The situation is saved by the queen who deals with it in a calm and dignified way.

She knows who should be consulted. 'She is the adult in court; she's the mature stateswoman'. This trope is a way in which those who are marginalized and powerless can express resistance and undermine their overlords.

Belshazzar's opening words to Daniel, reminding him that he is a Judean exile, seem something of slight and suggest that he had prior knowledge of him, since the queen had not mentioned this. Maybe he had deliberately ignored him, perhaps in a reaction against those his 'father' had favoured. Now he is forced to seek his service and even offers him a reward for them. Daniel curtly rejects the offer.

Daniel's long prologue to giving the interpretation is an indictment of the king. It is divided into two parts by the Aramaic word *'ant* (you) at the start of vv. 18 and 22. First he describes Nebuchadnezzar's greatness and power. He failed to realize that these were given to him by the Most High God and had to learn this by bitter experience. In the second part Daniel sternly rebukes Belshazzar. He has failed to learn the lesson he should have from his 'father's' experience and repeated his sin of arrogance. He has desecrated the vessels from the Jerusalem Temple. He has worshipped gods which 'do not see or hear or know'. He has failed to honour the God who has power over his life and destiny. This is the one place in the book where Daniel sounds like the Hebrew prophets who confronted the kings of Israel and Judah. Daniel then interprets the writing by means of a form of word-play in which he makes use of the verbal root that underlies each of the nouns he reads on the wall. The result is a declaration of God's judgement on Belshazzar and his reign. God has found him morally wanting and so his rule will be broken and his kingdom will pass to others.

Some commentators are puzzled that Belshazzar rewards Daniel after his sharp rebuke. It may be explicable in terms of his not wanting to lose face in public by breaking his promise. Even more find it puzzling that Daniel accepts the reward having curtly refused it. There is little consensus about this.

This story presents the fall of the Babylonian Empire as an act of divine judgement on an arrogant and sacrilegious king. It provides an example of what is said of the Most High God in the previous story, that he gives kingdoms 'to whom he will' (Dan 4:17). For the original hearers and readers, it would cohere with the more general prophecies of judgement on Babylon by the Hebrew prophets (e.g. Isa 13; Jer 50, 51) because Belshazzar exemplified some of the characteristics of the Empire as a whole. The queen's praise of Daniel, his recognition by Nebuchadnezzar and, even unwillingly, by Belshazzar, might encourage them to aspire to be like him.

Daniel 6

Here, as in Dan 3, the conflict arises primarily from professional envy. The fact that the conspirators seeking to bring Daniel down say, 'We shall not find any ground for complaint against this Daniel unless we find it in connection with the law of his God' is simply a witness to the fact that his professional integrity is such that it leaves no option but to look to some other area of his life in order to attack him. The way they refer to him in v. 13 may indicate some resentment towards him as a foreigner. King Darius is presented as well disposed towards Daniel. Like Nebuchadnezzar and Belshazzar, he is prone to pride. It is this that seems to predispose him to enact the flattering edict which the conspirators propose. Ironically, thinking that it declares his greatness and ability to do as he pleases, he finds himself trapped by his own decree in having to do something he never intended, and does not want to do.

When he hears of the decree, Daniel does not change his usual practice of prayer. For Jews in the Diaspora, unable to take part in the sacrificial worship in Jerusalem, the practice of prayer took on added importance (cf. Ps 141:2, 'Let my prayer be counted as incense before you, and the lifting up of my hands as an evening sacrifice'). There is reference to prayer at 'evening and morning and at noon' in Ps 55:17 but it is not until the Mishnah (m. Ber. 4.1) that there is clear evidence in Judaism of prayer being prescribed for these times. In Solomon's prayer in 1 Kgs 8 there is repeated mention of praying facing the land, Jerusalem and the Temple. In Tob 3:11–12 Sarah prays to God by a window saying, 'I turn my face to you'. Daniel is not openly confrontational but neither does he hide what he is doing. Because he prays at an open window his enemies have no difficulty in verifying that he is defying the king's decree. It is an open act of passive resistance.

The reason for Darius' distress when he is told of this is unclear. Was he angry with himself for having been tricked into causing Daniel's downfall? Is he angry with the conspirators for their manipulation of him? Is he angry with Daniel? Nor are we told exactly why he wants to save Daniel. His attitude contrasts with that of Nebuchadnezzar in Dan 3. He defied any god to deliver the three young men from the furnace. Darius expresses hope that Daniel's God will deliver him from the lions. As with the young men in ch. 3, Daniel is not only delivered from the lions' den, he is kept safe in it. When he is delivered Darius applies the law of *lex talionis* ('an eye for an eye, a tooth for a tooth'), which was widely accepted in the ancient Near East, to the conspirators so that they suffer the fate they intended for Daniel. The inclusion of their families may reflect the idea of corporate responsibility though, as Goldingay (2019: 317) points out, it 'raises logistical problems'. Their inclusion may be due to the hyperbole used in popular stories.

Daniel's practice of prayer is obviously another line that he is not prepared to cross in his critical engagement with a foreign culture. Why is this? In part it was probably a matter of personal integrity. His piety was well known and to stop praying or to pray in secret would be to compromise. But there is a deeper reason. Prayer has been mentioned previously in Dan 2:17–18 when Daniel tells his companions to 'seek mercy from the God of heaven' concerning Nebuchadnezzar's forgotten dream and its interpretation. This expresses their dependence on, and trust in, God. Daniel's faithfulness to, and trust in, his God is stressed in this story (vv. 16, 20, 23). In previous stories his special abilities are attributed to him being 'endowed with the spirit of the holy gods' (4:9; 5:11, 13). This story presents prayer as an important spiritual discipline which enables faithful service of God under the pressure of living in a foreign culture. In the two stories of 'court conflict' the moral and spiritual character of the Jewish exiles is at least as important as the act of deliverance.

Sovereignty: Divine and human (1)

Daniel 1:1–2 introduces a major theme of Daniel, the question of sovereignty. A natural way to understand Nebuchadnezzar's success in capturing Jerusalem and taking the vessels from the Temple to Babylon would have been that it demonstrated the power of Nebuchadnezzar's god(s) over the God of Israel. (cf. Sennacherib's words in 2 Kgs 18:33–35). The author of Daniel, however, asserts that his success was because the God of Israel 'gave' (*wayyittēn*) the Judean king and the temple vessels into Nebuchadnezzar's 'hand'. This was in accord with the prophecies of the pre-exilic prophets, including those in Jer 25:11–12; 29:10 alluded to in Dan 9:2. This raises the issues of which god is sovereign and of the relationship between divine sovereignty and human sovereignty.

The most direct treatment of these issues in the stories is in the doxologies which they contain. As noted above, in 2:20–23 Daniel declares that the God of Israel is omniscient and that he 'changes times and seasons, deposes and sets up kings'. Clearly human sovereignty is subordinate to his and is in his gift. Nebuchadnezzar's dream of the great statue reveals that this God has a purpose for human history, to 'set up a kingdom that shall never be destroyed, nor shall this kingdom be left to another people' (2:44). Nebuchadnezzar confesses that Daniel's God is 'God of gods and Lord of kings' (2:47). The deliverance of the three young men from the furnace answers the king's question, 'who is the god who can deliver you out of my hands?' He issues a decree threatening severe punishment of anyone who blasphemes the God of Shadrach, Meshach and Abednego.

Nebuchadnezzar's experience recounted in Dan 4 is intended to demonstrate to all who live 'that the Most High is sovereign over the kingdom of mortals; he gives it to whom he will' (4:17). At the end of it he confesses that the Most High lives for ever and that his sovereignty is everlasting and extols his omnipotence (4:35). It is important that he adds that he extols the King of heaven 'for all his works are truth, and his ways are justice; and he is able to bring low those who walk in pride' (4:37). The rule of the Most High is morally determined, not a matter of the arbitrary use of power. It is because of his pride (5:23) and because he is found morally wanting (5:27) that Belshazzar is stripped of his kingdom and his life. After Daniel is preserved from the lions, Darius sends a decree to everyone in his realm that they should 'tremble and fear before the God of Daniel: For he is the living God, enduring forever. His kingdom shall never be destroyed, and his dominion has no end. He delivers and rescues, he works signs and wonders in heaven and earth' (6:25–27).

The stories, therefore, present the God of Daniel, Shadrach, Meshach and Abednego as the Most High who is sovereign over all gods and kings. He is omnipotent and omniscient. His rule endures for ever and is characterized by truth and justice. He bestows sovereignty on human kings and has a plan for history. So, what is the nature of human sovereignty? There is ambiguity in the presentation of human rule by the image of the great tree in Dan 4. On the one hand it presents a picture in which the king provides security and sustenance so that those under his rule flourish. However, as noted in ch. 3, the image of a lofty tree is used in Ezek 17, 19, 31 of rulers whose pride leads to their downfall, as happens to Nebuchadnezzar. There is a difference in his case because he comes to admit his error and has his rule restored. This suggests that rulers can become rightful agents of God's rule for the good of those under their sovereignty. There are some, though, like Belshazzar who will not learn the lesson that they must recognize God's sovereignty and whose arrogance then leads to their final downfall. In Dan 2, all the kingdoms have been given their sovereignty by God (2:21) but they are of varying quality. What is said of the head of gold has obvious resonance with what is said about the tree in Dan 4 – it is apparently an appropriate rule over humans, wild animals and birds of the air. The reader is not told in what way the second kingdom is 'inferior' to the first. The fourth kingdom wreaks destruction. Human sovereignty is therefore presented as ambiguous. It can be for the great benefit of those ruled when the king recognizes that his sovereignty is granted by God and, like God's rule, is marked by truth and justice. When, perhaps because of their success, they become arrogant and act as if they were God, their rule causes harm to their subjects. Overall, the stories present the hearers and readers with a hopeful picture. Human rulers are fallible, given to pride in particular. As a result, critical engagement in a foreign realm will sometimes call for risky defiance of the king. However, trust in the ultimate sovereignty of their God should give them the confidence to persevere in that engagement with the hope of some measure of success in witnessing to the Most High as the God of gods and Lord of kings.

The ultimacy of God's rule is underlined by the end of the dream in Dan 2 where a stone 'cut out, not by human hands' breaks the statue in pieces and becomes a mountain which fills the whole earth (vv. 34–35). This seems to symbolize the replacement of Gentile kingdoms by God's kingdom in some form. Some see this as a later apocalyptic addition to the dream account. However, the smashing of Gentile kingdoms and their replacement by God's rule exercised through the Davidic king is part of the pre-exilic ideology of kingship in Judah, as evidenced by Pss 2 and 110 and Isa 11:1–9.

The rise of a post-colonial approach to the reading of texts has led to a fresh debate about the nature of the stories in Dan 1–6. Are they to be understood as basically 'accommodationist' in their stance? To what extent does the form of 'lifestyle for diaspora' that they encourage lead the Jewish exiles to accept their position as 'colonised people' and give legitimacy to the imperial power? Over against such a reading some scholars have argued that the stories express hostility to imperial power and encourage strong resistance to it (e.g. Smith-Christopher, 1996, 20–1). These argue that the kings are presented as insecure and fearful, slow on the uptake to the point of stupidity, prone to irrational rages and readily manipulated by their courtiers. Also, the irony that runs through the stories is a form of humiliation. Newsom (2014: 15–18) argues that it is not a simple matter of either accommodation or resistance. There is a more complex dialogue going on in the stories. Their authors adopt the court tale genre from the dominant culture but adapt it for their own purpose. Ethnic and religious tensions are introduced. There is, as discussed above, a sustained theological reflection on the relationship between divine and human sovereignty which tends to subvert the imperial claims to power and destabilize it. In particular Newsom concludes (2014: 17) that, 'the confessions placed in the mouths of the Gentile kings in Dan 1-6 are to be seen neither as merely accommodation nor resistance but as attempts to negotiate the ideological double bind of life under Persian rule' (*see also*: Pace, 2008: 5–6).

Daniel 7–12: The pressure of persecution

Daniel 7

The chiastic arrangement of Dan 2–7 puts the visions of a sequence of four kingdoms in chs 2 and 7 in parallel. There is, however, a change in the 'feel' of the imagery from positive to negative. In ch. 2 the kingdoms are depicted by a human figure but in ch. 7 they are depicted as bizarre beasts. If what is suggested above in ch. 3 about the probable Babylonian background of the imagery is valid, these are chaos monsters and ominous portents. Whereas in ch. 2 the fourth kingdom 'crushes and smashes everything' the language is stronger in ch. 7 where the fourth best is described as 'terrifying and dreadful and exceedingly strong' and it devours, breaks in pieces and stamps on what is left. Out of it comes a little horn that speaks arrogantly. The evil nature of these beastly kingdoms is underlined in the following throne scene in which they are judged and condemned by the Ancient One. The climax of the vision is the investiture of the 'one like a human being' with universal and everlasting glory and kingship. The interpretation identifies this as the kingdom that is given to '(the people of) the holy ones of the Most High' (7:18, 27). This corresponds to the setting up by God of a universal and everlasting kingdom, symbolized by the 'stone cut from the mountain not by hands' at the end of the vision in ch. 2. In ch. 2 nothing is said about the process that this will involve. However, in ch. 7 it is made clear that there is going to be great suffering before the kingdom is established. The little horn will make war on the holy ones and prevail over them for a period (v. 21). He will wear them out as he tries to change their 'sacred seasons and the law' but this suffering will last for only a limited period (v. 25). There is no indication that the 'everlasting kingdom' will be brought in by any human militaristic action. It is bestowed on 'the people of the holy ones of the Most High' by a legal decision of the heavenly court (v. 26–27).

In this vision the world appears as a much more hostile place than it does in the stories. In particular there is the warning that those faithful to the

Most High will face severe persecution because of their adherence to their religion. As an encouragement to endure through this they are assured that it will be for a limited period because the Most High is sovereign over human rulers and the little horn will face divine judgement and lose his dominion. Everlasting dominion will be given to those who remain faithful as the holy ones of the Most High.

Daniel 8

The vision of the ram and the he-goat provides further details of the period of persecution foretold in the previous vision. The he-goat is identified as 'the king of Greece' who conquered the Persian Empire (vv. 20–21). He is Alexander the Great. The little horn is a king who will arise out of the break-up of Alexander's empire. The detailed understanding of what is said about his actions against 'the beautiful land' (Palestine) in vv. 10–12 is a matter of considerable debate. A minority see v. 10 as a way of referring to the Jewish people, seen as 'heavenly' because of their relationship with God. Most think that, in the context of the Hebrew Bible, the language is best understood as pointing to a transcendent dimension to the conflict between the little horn and the Jews. One of the epithets of the God of Israel is 'YHWH of hosts' and the Song of Deborah speaks of the stars fighting from heaven on behalf of Israel (Judg 5:20). The question then is whether the 'host' in v. 11 is still the heavenly host, in which case the 'prince' (nāgîd) might be the angel Michael (Dan 10:21, though here the word śar is used for 'prince'), or has its meaning changed to refer to the Jews, with the High Priest being the 'prince' (nāgîd can be used of a senior priest, including the High Priest, for example, 2 Chron 35:8)? The Hebrew of v.12a is difficult to construe and again there is debate about the referent of 'the host' – does it refer to the Jews or to the army that attacks them? This leads to different understandings of the 'wickedness'. Is it the wickedness of the attackers or of the Jews? What is clear is that the little horn desecrates the sanctuary and stops the regular sacrificial offerings. The 'truth' he casts 'to the ground' is no doubt the Jewish Torah. There is general agreement that this refers to the persecution of the Jews in Judea by the Seleucid king Antiochus IV in 167–164 BCE.

Daniel overhears a discussion between two heavenly beings which raises the question of how long this persecution will last (v. 13). This echoes the question, 'How long?' which occurs in the psalms of lament (e.g. Pss 74:9–10; 79:5; 80:4 [MT 80:5]) and also in the prophets (Zech 1:12 is a close parallel in that it is a call for God's mercy on Jerusalem and Judea). Commentators disagree over whether 'two thousand three hundred evenings and mornings' (v. 14) refers to this number of days, or to the regular evening and morning sacrifices in the temple, and so to half that number of days. In either case, no one has been able to explain satisfactorily of the significance of the number. However, there is the assurance that it will last for a limited, relatively short, period.

Gabriel's interpretation of the vision (vv. 19–26) makes two further points that would be of some comfort to the persecuted Jews. The first is the implication that God is in control of this 'period of wrath'. This is implied in the phrase 'the appointed time of the end' (v. 19) because the one doing the 'appointing' must be the God of Israel. Then there is the phrase 'But he shall be broken, and not by human hands' (v. 25) which echoes what is said about the stone in Dan 2:34. 45. This indicates that God will bring an end to the little horn's career. The second is the reason given for the delay in ending the period of wrath in v. 23a. This takes up what is said in Gen 15:16 about God delaying action against 'the Amorites' in Canaan until their wickedness grew so that it was plainly obvious that they deserved punishment (cf. Lev 18:25). Judgement is delayed so that when it is carried out it is seen to be justly administered. The delay is not due to God's inability to act. This argument is applied specifically to the experience of suffering under Antiochus IV in 2 Macc 6:14–16,

> For in the case of other nations the Lord waits patiently to punish them until they reach full measure of their sins; but he does not deal this way with us, in order that he may not take vengeance on us afterward when our sins have reached their height. Therefore he never withdraws his mercy from us. Though he disciplines us with calamities, he does not forsake his own people.

Daniel 9

The debate about the origins of this prayer has been discussed in ch. 2. Whatever conclusion one comes to about that, its inclusion here underlines the message of Dan 1:1–2. The prayer makes it clear that the destruction of Jerusalem and its Temple, and the subsequent exile was not due to YHWH's inability to defend his people. They were the result of YHWH's action in accordance with the Mosaic Covenant and the curses attached to breaking it, as the pre-exilic prophets had warned would happen (vv. 10–11). So, the prayer is one of confession and repentance. It is also a prayer of supplication, a prayer of hope. Its hope is not based on what the Judeans deserve but on the nature of YHWH (v. 18). He is great and awesome (v. 4), righteous (vv. 7, 16), merciful and forgiving (v. 9). There is another basis for the supplication, namely that YHWH should act, 'for your own sake, O my God, because your city and your people bear your name' (v. 19). In the eyes of the nations YHWH's reputation is bound up with that of Jerusalem and the Judeans.

The appearance of the supernatural messenger Gabriel gives assurance that the supplication has been heard and received favourably. Daniel is told that a word has gone out (by implication, from God) that certain things will happen within a fixed period of 'seventy weeks' (generally taken to mean 'seventy weeks of years' as in Lev 25:8; *see* Excursus 1 in ch. 2). The overall outcome of this period is summed up in v. 24 in six phrases. Three are negative, using words for wrongdoings that will be brought to an end: transgression, sin and iniquity. Commentators disagree as to whether these refer to Israel's sins, such as those confessed in the prayer (v. 5) or to the evil deeds of Antiochus IV. Since in Dan 11:30–35; 12:10 there is reference to Jews who supported Antiochus, the reference may be to both (so, Porteus, 1979: 141). The first of the positive phrases, 'to bring in everlasting righteousness (*ṣedeq*)' is usually taken as referring to the establishing of YHWH's rule (the same word has been used of YHWH in vv. 7, 14, 16). The second phrase about 'sealing' the 'vision and prophet' suggests the authentication of Jeremiah's prophecy by its fulfilment. The final clause refers to the rededication of the Jerusalem Temple and may contain an allusion back to Dan 8:13–14.

The prayer reminds the hearers and readers of Daniel that YHWH remains faithful to his covenant with Israel and asserts that he is a 'great and awesome God'. Once again, the persecuted Jews are assured that their God, is in control of events and that their time of suffering, which reaches a climax in the last of the seventy weeks, will be for a short period only. This should encourage them to remain faithful and endure until 'the decreed end' (v. 27).

Daniel 10–12

The possible implication in Dan 8:10 that there is a transcendent dimension to events on Earth is made explicit in the epiphany vision in Dan 10:10–11:1, where it is also asserted that there is a synergism between events in these two realms. This view of things is not something new in Daniel. It is rooted in the Hebrew Bible, in which it is assumed that events on Earth, especially battles, are influenced by heavenly involvement. It is particularly clear when heavenly forces are said to come to the aid of Israel to enable them to defeat their enemies (e.g. Num 10:35–36; Deut 33:2–3; Judg 5:19–20; Hab 3:12–13). The notion that each nation is under the care of a particular god was common in the ancient Near East, and is expressed in Deut 32:8–9. Ben Sirach (*Sirach* 17:17) took this to mean that YHWH appointed a different heavenly being to rule over each nation but that YHWH himself rules over Israel. In Dan 10:21 it is Michael, rather than YHWH, who is the heavenly guardian of Israel.

Within the survey of history in 11:2–45, the careers of four kings stand out: the 'warrior king' (vv. 3–4); the 'king of the north' of vv. 10–19; the king of v. 20; and the 'contemptible person' (vv. 21–45). Because of the amount of space given to him, the last person is the focus of the survey. Some aspects of his career are foreshadowed by those of the earlier kings. Like the warrior king and king of the north he is able to 'do as he pleases' (vv. 3, 16, 36). Like the king of the north, he invades 'the beautiful land' (vv. 16, 41) and gains some support there (vv. 14, 30, 32). Both make treacherous agreements (vv. 17, 23) and meet a check to their rise to power (vv. 18, 30). The king of the north shows some hint of the arrogance of the contemptible person (vv. 12, 36, 37). Like the king of v. 20, the contemptible person is concerned with exacting tribute and gathering wealth (vv. 28, 43). This foreshadowing prepares the hearers and readers for the fact that despite the much greater success of the contemptible person, his career, like theirs, will come to an untimely end (vv. 4, 19, 20). This 'patterning' of history points to a moral force at work in it, which they would recognize as God's judgement.

The message of this view of history is that there will be times when evil is rampant and there is great suffering because there are heavenly powers, and human rulers related to them, who can and do oppose God. They may have a measure of success for a time. However, there is no ultimate dualism. God is sovereign and is somehow in control even when evil is dominant. God's plans and purposes will prevail. The faithful are therefore given encouragement to stand firm and not to yield to the temptation, as some do, to side with the evil-doers (vv. 30, 32). There is no attempt here to resolve the dilemma of affirming God's sovereignty over history in the face of evil, even persecution of God's people. There is only the challenge to live by trust in God despite the tension that produces.

A further encouragement to stand firm, even in the face of death, is given in Dan 12:1–3. This contains the only clear affirmation of belief in resurrection of the dead in the Hebrew Bible. The language of resurrection is used metaphorically in Hos 6:2 of the revival of the nation, 'After two days he will revive us; on the third day he will raise us up, that we may live before him'. The vivid picture of dry bones coming to life as living human beings in Ezek 37 is also metaphorical, as v. 11 makes clear, 'these bones are the whole house of Israel'. It is referring to the return from exile and the re-establishment of the nation in its homeland. The exact meaning if Isa 26:19–21 is unclear. Some see it as an expression of hope for individual resurrection. Others take it in the same metaphorical sense as Ezek 37. There is disagreement about the significance of the word 'many' in Dan 12:2. In Hebrew רַבִּים (*rabbîm*) can be used in the sense of 'all' when the stress is on the numbers involved, so some see here a reference to universal resurrection. However, the following preposition *min* is most naturally taken in its partitive sense, meaning that only some of those who sleep will wake. The context (11:33–35; 12:3) suggests that these are the martyred faithful Jews. They will enjoy 'everlasting life'. Those who face 'everlasting contempt' are presumably their persecutors. This promise of resurrection and post-mortem vindication would give people good reason to remain faithful to God under persecution.

Sovereignty: Divine and human (2)

The clearest presentation of divine sovereignty in Dan 7–12 is the throne scene in 7:9–14 and its interpretation in 7:26–27. God, described as 'an Ancient One', who is enthroned in the midst of his myriad of attendants, carries out judgement on the beasts that represent human rulers, and bestows 'dominion and glory and kingship' on 'one like a human being' who in some way represents 'the people of the holy of the Most High'. This clearly depicts divine sovereignty over human rulers and human history. There are intimations of this in the vision of the beasts. There is debate about the meaning of what is done to the first beast in v. 4b. The echoes of Dan 4 recall the judgement on Nebuchadnezzar's hubris and so the meaning may be that the whole of his dynasty stands under the same judgement of God (so Collins, 1993, 298). The significance of the command 'Arise, devour many bodies!' given to the second beast (v. 5) is also debatable but may be a reminder of the prophecies that YHWH will stir up the Medes to attack Babylon (Isa 13:13; Jer 51:11, 28). There is also the statement that dominion 'was given' to the third beast (v. 6). These are reminders that God is there in the background as the 'Lord of kings' (2:47). The prolonging of the lives of the first three beasts (v. 12) puzzles those seeking a historical interpretation of it, but the point of it may be theological: God's judgement is discriminating and just. The fourth beast is dealt with differently because of its greater offences. The references in Dan 8 to the great horn of the male goat being broken (v. 8) and of there being an 'appointed time of the end' (v. 19) when the little horn will be broken 'not by human hands' (v. 25) are also reminders of divine sovereignty at work in human history.

In the prayer in Dan 9 YHWH is described as 'great and awesome' and it is made clear that the destruction of Jerusalem and the temple was the result of his judgement on Israel because they were unfaithful to the covenant, not because of Babylonian power. However, as noted above, the main emphasis is on YHWH's moral character. The assertion that seventy weeks 'are decreed' (v. 24) is a reminder of YHWH's sovereignty over history. This is underlined in the lengthy survey of history that is presented in Dan 10–12.

The presentation of history as prophecy from the contents of 'the book of truth' in Dan 11:2–12:4 affirms the belief that history is under God's control and in some sense determined by God. This, however, does not necessarily mean that history is fully pre-scripted with all the actors carrying out the roles set for them like puppets. The Prince of Persia can oppose and delay what God intends, and there is a relationship between this heavenly figure and the human ruler of Persia. The correlation between the three weeks of Daniel's prayer and the three-week delay before the messenger who set out at the beginning of his prayer can break free, with Michael's help, suggests that human prayer has its effect on the events concerned. Three of the kings in the historical survey are said to do as they please (vv. 3, 16, 36), implying a measure of freedom in their actions. Also, people are held to account for their actions since they are said to act wickedly or wisely and this can have eternal consequences (12:2). On the other hand, phrases like 'he will be broken' (v. 20) and references to 'an appointed time' and 'the end' (vv. 29, 35) are reminders that God is in control.

The visions in Dan 7–12 present a more negative view of human sovereignty than that found in the stories of Dan 1–6. The bestial imagery in Dan 7:1–8, especially in contrast to the image of the 'one like a human being', would evoke for Jewish readers the creation account in Gen 1:26–28 where humans, because they are made in God's image and likeness, are given dominion over the beasts. This is clearly echoed in Ps 8:5–8. Also significant is Ps 32:8–9 where those who refuse to accept and follow God's instruction and follow his way are compared to 'a horse or mule, without understanding, whose temper must be curbed with bit and bridle'. The stories hold out the possibility that human rulers may *image* God and so have the right and ability to rule in his name. However, they also hold out the warning that when rulers try to *be* God, they forfeit that right and face judgement. The picture in Dan 7:1–8 is of rulers who have done this and so have become bestial. This negative view is enhanced if, as argued in ch. 3, the imagery is drawn from the Babylonian creation epic and the beasts reflect the chaos monsters in it.

Portier-Young (2011: 181) notes the significance of the reference to Antiochus' attempt to 'change the sacred seasons and the law (7:25b, cf. 11; 11:31b). She says, 'Inherent in the effort to change the calendar, halt regular religious practices, and replace them with new ones was an attempt to deny the sovereignty of the God the Jews worshipped and to co-opt their time-consciousness into an alternately constructed reality'.

When discussing in Chapter 1 the use of two languages in Daniel we noted the suggestion by post-colonial interpreters that it is a way of signalling the decisive change brought about by Antiochus' edict and calling their readers to reject his sovereignty and adhere to the covenant with their God.

The promise of the throne scene and its interpretation is that one day God's original purpose for humans will be achieved and a kingdom established with dominion over the world in which there is a rule which truly images God. It is striking that there is no hint that this rule will be exercised by a descendant of King David. Does this reflect the view expressed in Isa 55:3–5 that the whole nation of Israel will assume the role given to the Davidic king of exercising God's rule in the world?

Excursus 3: Resistance in Daniel and 1 Maccabees

When Cyrus took over the Babylonian Empire, he encouraged the peoples whom the Babylonians had taken into exile to return to their homelands to live by their traditional customs, laws and religion. This is attested to in the Cyrus Cylinder and, with regard to the Judeans, in Ezra 1:1–4. As long as they paid their taxes, lived peacefully, obeyed their local Governor, and whatever edicts Cyrus did make, they had considerable local autonomy.

There is no evidence that Alexander's conquest of Palestine had much effect on affairs in Jerusalem. After Alexander's death his generals were primarily concerned about establishing their own power bases. When

Ptolemy gained control of Egypt and Palestine, he seems to have left the situation in Jerusalem and Judea much as it had been under the Persians. There is no evidence that his successors changed things very much. Judea was affected by the periodic disruptions cause by conflicts between the Ptolemies and Seleucids. Rifts developed in Jerusalem between pro-Ptolemaic and pro-Seleucid factions. When the Seleucid ruler Antiochus III eventually gained control of Palestine in 198 BCE, he confirmed the right of the Jews to live by their ancestral laws and customs. During this period about thirty Greek cities were founded in Palestine and the Trans-Jordan area. Some were new foundations and others were based on existing cities. As the political and economic influence of these cities grew there was an increasing desire among some of the upper classes in Jerusalem to adapt their lifestyle to that of the Hellenistic upper classes of these cities. A faction grew up that wanted to found a Greek city within Jerusalem. Others opposed this strenuously as a threat to their ancestral ways and religion.

Following the humiliating terms of the Peace of Apamea in 188 BCE Antiochus III and his successors took greater interest in the local affairs within what remained of their empire. They needed to maximize their tax revenue given the parlous state of their finances due to the huge indemnity that they had to pay to Rome. There was also concern to prevent the rise of any national independence movements inspired by the weakening of Seleucid power following their defeat. After Antiochus' death in 187, while robbing a temple in Elam, his son Seleucus IV succeeded him. With the support of some pro-Hellenistic Jews, he sent his chief minister, Heliodorus, to expropriated private funds that were deposited in the temple for safe keeping. This attempt was unsuccessful but led to open factionalism in Jerusalem. Some pro-Hellenists accused the High Priest, Onias III, of being pro-Ptolemy. When, following Seleucus' murder, Antiochus IV came to power the pro-Hellenists persuaded him to depose Onias III and replace him by his brother Jason. This was contrary to the accepted practice that the High Priest held office for life. The High Priest was the tax-collector and Jason promised to pay a bigger revenue to the king. The pro-Hellenists also got Antiochus' agreement to the founding of a Greek city in Jerusalem named 'Antioch' after him. The traditionalists in Jerusalem were outraged. The outrage grew when Menelaus, by offering an even higher tax-return bid, got Antiochus to depose Jason and put himself in the office. Because Menelaus was not an Aaronite, in the view of the orthodox Jews he was not qualified to be High Priest. He compounded the situation by having Onias

III murdered. On his way back from his first campaign in Egypt, in 169, Antiochus plundered the temple in Jerusalem with Menelaus' connivance. Intervention by the Roman Senate, to whom the Egyptians had appealed for help, forced Antiochus to end his second campaign in 167 with a humiliating retreat. On his way home he heard that there was unrest in Jerusalem. This was due to fighting between the rival factions there but Antiochus took it to mean an uprising against himself. He sent an army to suppress it and build and garrison a citadel, called the Acra, in Jerusalem. It was constituted as a Greek city and housed renegade Jews as well as non-Jews. Antiochus decided to deal with the intransigence of the orthodox Jewish by outlawing traditional Jewish religious practices: reading the Torah, keeping the Sabbath, practising circumcision, observing the food laws and offering Jewish sacrifices in the temple. The temple was rededicated to Zeus/Jupiter, whose image was set up in it, and swine flesh was offered on the altar of burnt offerings.

1 Maccabees 1–2 describes the fierce persecution of faithful Jews which ensued and the start of the Maccabean rebellion. These chapters present four responses to the persecution. One was to accept the outlawing of traditional practices and to offer sacrifice to Zeus. Some who did this had already decided to assimilate to Hellenistic culture. No doubt others were coerced to do so because of the threat of death. According to 1 Macc 2:29, 'many who were seeking righteousness and justice went down to the wilderness to live there'. These tried to withdraw into a safe place and follow the traditional practices without publicly defying the laws. However, Antiochus' officers in Jerusalem heard of some of these and surrounded them on a sabbath day. When they refused either to surrender or fight, they were massacred. Hearing of this, the Maccabees and their followers, who had also fled to the wilderness, decided to take up arms against the Seleucid forces and renegade Jews and fight even on the sabbath if necessary (1 Macc 2:39–41). They were joined by a group called 'Hasideans' (or 'Hasidim') who are described as 'mighty warriors of Israel, all who offered themselves willingly for the law' (1 Macc 2:42). A few years later this group split with the Maccabees. After Antiochus IV's death, Demetrius I gained the throne. He replaced Menelaus as High Priest by an Aaronite called Alcimus. While the Maccabees refused to make peace with the Seleucids, the Hasideans did so because Alcimus was qualified for the office. This suggests that their goal was restoration of the traditional religious practices. The Maccabees seemed set on more than this, on making Judea an independent state.

1 Maccabees was written to support the legitimacy of the Hasmonean priesthood which was established by the Maccabees. They are the heroes of the book and the author presents the 'manifesto' of their revolt in the words of Mattathias reported in 2:27, 40–41, 50. Here zeal for the law and defence of the covenant is equated with active, violent, resistance against the forces of Antiochus.

Most commentators agree that **Dan 11:21–45** refers to the career of Antiochus IV and that vv. 29–35 refer to his persecution of the Jews. The Hellenistic Jews who colluded with Antiochus' actions are described as 'those who forsake the holy covenant' (v. 30) and 'those who violate the covenant' (v. 32a). In contrast to these are 'the people who are loyal to their God and stand firm and take action' (v. 32b). But what kind of 'action' is the author commending? There is no explicit mention of armed resistance to overcome the persecutors. Indeed, the reference to Antiochus IV's end in Dan 8:25, 'but he shall be broken, and not by human hands' suggests that this is not the kind of action envisaged but that the author is expecting some direct divine action that will mean 'he shall come to his end, with no one to help him' (v. 45). In Dan 7 that divine action is a judicial verdict leading to the establishment of the 'everlasting kingdom' with no suggestion of any human militaristic action. Nor does the author suggest some kind of withdrawal and keeping of the covenant laws in secret, such as some attempted to do according to 1 Macc 2:29. Instead, he commends the actions of 'the wise' (vv. 33–35). These seem to be learned Jews who instruct others in the covenant law and encourage them to stand firm in it, not in secret but openly, even to the point of martyrdom. He is commending a form of non-violent public resistance such as we've seen modelled in Dan 3 and 6. In the course of this some of the wise themselves will set an example by suffering martyrdom. In Dan 12:3 the wise are described as 'those who lead many to righteousness'. Some commentators (*see* Lucas, 2002: 287, 295, 303; Portier-Young, 2011, 272–6) see in this phrase an allusion to Isa 53:11. This is in the last of the so-called 'Servant Songs' in Isa 40–55. These speak of the Servant's faithful involvement in God's mission to the world despite rejection, suffering and death. Isa 52:13–53:12 affirms that the Servant will be vindicated and enjoy his reward, even beyond death. In ch. 5 we will consider attempts to identify who 'the wise' were.

There has been much debate about the phrase in 11:34, 'they [the wise] shall receive a little help, and many shall join them insincerely'. Most scholars see it as a rather disparaging reference to the activities of the Maccabees and those who 'join them insincerely' as referring to those who joined the Maccabees out of fear because of the reprisals that the Maccabees took against those they regarded as renegade Jews. Against this is the absence of explicit support elsewhere in Daniel for armed resistance to persecution. Alternatively, this verse may mean that only a few will genuinely share the 'understanding' imparted by 'the wise' and give them wholehearted support (Newsom, 2014, 353).

Portier-Young (2011: 262) sums up what she sees as the kinds of non-violent resistance advocated by the book of Daniel as modelled by its heroes,

> studying the scriptures … humbling themselves, including fasting, prayer, and penitence; teaching God's message to the people; defying the decrees of Antiochus and preserving practices of the faith even at the cost of their lives; giving an example to others; and giving strength to others.

5

Daniel: When, who and where?

The date of the Book of Daniel

In the latter part of the second century CE an anti-Christian writer, Porphyry, argued that Daniel was written in the second century BCE. A number of Christian scholars responded to him, including Jerome who preserves much of Porphyry's argumentation in his commentary on Daniel, written in 407 CE. From then on there was a general acceptance that Daniel was written in the sixth century BCE until this began to be questioned in the eighteenth century CE. Throughout the following century there was heated debate over the book's date of composition. By the early twentieth century a consensus had been reached among most scholars in favour of a Maccabean date for the final form of the book, but some have continued to defend a sixth-century date. We will briefly survey the main areas of debate.

The languages of Daniel

These were discussed in Chapter 1. There it was suggested that the evidence of the Persian and Greek loan-words was 'neutral' with regard to dating the book. The Aramaic falls between that of the fourth-century Samaritan papyri and the second-century Qumran documents, while the Hebrew is more like that of Chronicles than the Qumran documents. Advocates of a sixth-century date for the book question the reliability of attempting to date it by its language because of the widespread area from which the evidence is drawn and the assumption that linguistic development would occur at a similar rate in different geographical and social contexts. In any case, the language of the final form of the book does not settle the issue of the date of the origin of the materials included in it.

Historical problems

There are a number of historical problems which have been seen as evidence that the author of the book must have been writing much later than the sixth century and have had limited knowledge of that period of history.

Daniel 1:1–2. Even before the modern debate, commentators were concerned about the problem that Jer 25:1 equates Nebuchadnezzar's first year with the fourth year of Jehoiakim's reign, whereas Dan 1:1 seems to equate it with the third year. Some modern scholars (e.g. Hasel, 1981) argue that the two writers are using different methods of reckoning the years of a king's reign. Jehoiakim was an Egyptian vassal and Jeremiah could be using the Egyptian convention in which the period between a king's accession and the next New Year was counted as 'year 1'. In Babylon, where the stories about Daniel were probably written, this period was counted as 'year 0' of the reign. Millard (1977: 69) has argued that if Dan 1:1 uses the Babylonian method of reckoning the years of a king's reign but an autumn New Year, as may have been the case in Judah, Jehoiakim's third year would then run into October 605. However, there is uncertainty about whether the New Year in pre-exilic Judah began in the spring month of Nisan or the autumn month of Tishri.

A bigger problem is whether Nebuchadnezzar did, or could have, besieged Jerusalem so early in his reign. The *Babylonian Chronicle* for this period has survived (Grayson, 1975: 99–100). Nebuchadnezzar led the Babylonian army which defeated the Egyptians at Carchemish in the summer of 605. He then conquered 'the whole region of Hamath' (northern Syria). Hearing of the death of his father, Nabopolassar, he returned to Babylon and acceded to the throne on 6/7 September 605. He then rejoined the army in the West to carry out operations in Hattu until the following Spring when he returned to Babylon to take part in the New Year Festival in Nisan 604. The *Chronicle* claims that as a result of the operations in Hattu, 'all the kings of Hattu came before him and he received their heavy tribute.' Wiseman (1985: 23) assumes that this included Jehoiakim of Judah, although Judah lay further south than the region normally referred to as Hattu (roughly modern Syria-Lebanon). If we accept the statement in 2 Kgs 24:1 that Jehoiakim paid tribute to Nebuchadnezzar for three years before rebelling, he must have made an act of submission at some point. A likely cause of his rebellion would be Nebuchadnezzar's failed attempt to invade Egypt in 601, giving 604–601 as the period of submission. However, there is no mention in the *Babylonian Chronicle* of Nebuchadnezzar besieging Jerusalem in this period.

However, as suggested in the discussion of Dan 2 in ch. 3, concentration on the historical details may not be appropriate with regard to a court story which is primarily concerned to entertain, educate and encourage its readers rather than providing a historical report. Its main point is theological, that whenever and however Nebuchadnezzar was able to take booty from Jerusalem and the temple, this was not due to the superiority of his god(s), but was brought about by a deliberate act of Judah's God.

The Median Empire. The prominence given to the Median Empire in Dan 2 and 7 has been seen by many as evidence of a lack of knowledge of the historical relationship of the Babylonian, Median and Persian empires, though some (e.g. Montgomery, 1927: 328; Heaton, 1956: 192) have questioned this view in light of Dan 8:3–4. When discussing the vision in Dan 7 in ch. 3 it was argued that the prominence given to the Median Empire is understandable if the viewpoint of the book of Daniel is that of Judean exiles in Mesopotamia rather than that of those in Judea.

Belshazzar. When discussing Dan 4 in ch. 3 it was noted that until 1854 there was no mention of Belshazzar in any extant ancient source other than Daniel. Since then, it has become clear that he was Nabonidus' son and heir and that when Nabonidus went to live in Teima he 'entrusted the kingship' in Babylon to Belshazzar (*Verse Account of Nabonidus 2.20, ANET* 313). Some have seen the use of the title 'king' (*melek*) of Belshazzar in Dan 5 as unhistorical because he seems not to have enjoyed some royal prerogatives, including the title *šarru*, 'king' (see Beaulieu, 1989: 185–203, where the royal prerogatives he did and did not enjoy are listed). A semantic resolution of this issue is suggested by a bilingual (Aramaic and Assyrian) inscription on a statue of the ninth-century ruler of Guzan discovered at Tell Fakhariyeh in Syria. In the Assyrian text he is styled *šakin guzani* (governor of Guzan) but in the Aramaic text he is styled as *mlk gwzn* (king of Guzan) (Millard and Bordreuil, 1982). This suggests that *mlk* in Aramaic had a wider meaning than *šarru* in Akkadian. If it was used of a governor of a province, it could be used of the Prince Regent.

In Dan 5 Nebuchadnezzar and Belshazzar are spoken of as father and son, whereas historically Belshazzar was the eldest son of Nabonidus. The language of father/son can be used loosely in the sense of ancestor/

descendant, but there is no clear evidence of any direct family relationship between Nebuchadnezzar and Belshazzar. The use of it here may not be the result of historical confusion. In discussing Dan 5 in ch. 4 it was suggested that the use of 'father' of Nebuchadnezzar rather than 'predecessor' is a literary device to enhance the contrast between him and Belshazzar.

Darius the Mede (Dan 5:31 [MT 6:1]; 6:28 [MT 6:29]; 9:1). Darius the Mede is not known from any extra-biblical source. Babylon was captured by the forces of Cyrus the Persian. The debate about Darius the Mede has been long, complicated and sometimes heated (Rowley, 1935, reviews the debate up to 1934). Four positions have been argued for.

In the late nineteenth and early twentieth centuries many scholars held the view that Darius the Mede was another name for the general who captured Babylon on behalf of Cyrus. Cuneiform sources refer to him as Ugbaru or Gubaru and in classical sources he is called Gobryas. Rowley (1935: 19–29) exposed the weakness of this view. He pointed out that there is no evidence that Ugbaru/Gubaru was ever called Darius; that he was a Mede; that he was the son of Ahasuerus; or that he bore the title of king. It later became clear that Ugbaru/Gubaru died very soon after capturing Babylon and that Cyrus' son Cambyses was 'king of Babylon' under his father for about a year after its capture (Grabbe, 1988).

A majority of scholars have come to regard Darius the Mede as a literary construct. The Hebrew prophets spoke of a Median conquest of Babylon (Isa 13:17; 21:2; Jer 51:11, 28). In Dan 2 and 7 the 'four kingdoms' scheme has a Median Empire between that of Babylon and Persia. Unaware of the actual course of history the writer of Daniel assumed a Median conquest of Babylon. The sequence of stories in Dan 1–6 therefore needed a Median king between Belshazzar and Cyrus the Persian (6:28 [MT 6:29]). Darius the Mede was created to meet this need.

Wiseman (1965) suggested that the key to Darius the Mede's identity is to be found in Dan 6:28 [MT 6:29]. It can be translated as, 'Daniel prospered in the reign of Darius, even (namely, or i.e.) the reign of Cyrus the Persian.' This takes the conjunction *waw* in this verse as explicative, as in 1 Chr 5:26, where this type of construction identifies 'Pul' with Tiglath-Pileser. Baker (1980) has shown that the explicative *waw* is well attested in Hebrew, Aramaic, Ugaritic and Akkadian. Wiseman went on to argue that since Cyrus had a Median mother and took over the Median Empire, he could be called a Mede, even 'king of the Medes.' Also, he would have been about sixty-two when he conquered Babylon. The statement that Darius' father was

Ahasuerus is problematic since Cyrus' father was named Cambyses. Wiseman suggests that 'Ahasuerus' might be an old Achaemenid royal name. Grabbe (1988: 207) dismisses Wiseman's proposal as depending too much on 'what could have been.'

Colless (1982) supports Wiseman's reading of Dan 6:28 [MT 6:29] from a literary standpoint. He notes that most of the major figures in Daniel have two (or more) names. He also argues that it is very unlikely that the author of Daniel was unaware of the biblical references to Cyrus as the conqueror of Babylon (e.g. Isa 45:1; 2 Chr 36:19–23; Ezra 1:1–4). He gives Cyrus the Persian the additional name 'Darius the Mede' because as a 'student of prophecy' (Dan 9:1–2) he knew that the Medes should play a part in the conquest of Babylon. Since Cyrus was partly Median and ruled the Medes as well as the Persians this was emphasized by giving him the name 'Darius the Mede.' So, according to Coxon, Darius the Mede is both a literary construct and a historical person.

Daniel and the apocalypses

Chapter 2 discussed the relationship between Daniel and Jewish apocalypses. It was noted that only Dan 10–12 fit the SBL Seminar's definition of an apocalypse. These chapters seem to be an early example of this genre of literature. The other known early examples are the Book of Watchers and the Astronomical Book which are now part of *1 Enoch*. They are usually dated to the early second, or even the late third century BCE. This suggests a similar date as the earliest possible date for the final form of Daniel.

The compilation and date of Daniel

In Chapter 1 the issues that have been the subject of debate in discussions of the compilation of Daniel have been surveyed and it was noted that no consensus has emerged with regard to the process of compilation.

The few modern advocates of a sixth-century date for the book take the author of the visions to be a Judean exile in Babylon. They usually then argue that this person is the sole author of the whole book, despite the third-person form of the stories, by stressing the existence of literary and theological similarities between the visions and the stories (e.g. Baldwin, 1978: 38–40). House (2018: 25–6), though, posits a single author who wrote the stories and incorporated the autobiographical vision reports. Most scholars see this as underplaying the theological tensions between the two parts of the book.

Those who argue for a second-century date of the book as we know it, because of the prominence in the visions of the career of Antiochus IV and his persecution of the Jews, generally accept that in the stories it incorporates material of earlier origin. Most scholars recognize that the ethos and content of the stories militates against them being originally composed in the second century. They give an authentic picture of life in an ancient Near Eastern court, especially a Persian one (e.g. Hartman & Di Lella, 1978: 13; Pace, 2008: 5–6) and the relationship they depict between the kings and faithful Judean exiles is too positive. The logic of accepting the case made by Humphreys (1973), as most do, that the stories commend 'a life style for Diaspora' is acceptance that they originated, and first circulated, among the diaspora and not among the persecuted Jews of Judea in the second century. Moreover, if the stories were originally composed to address Jews during the Antiochene persecution, it is surprising that they do not raise two of the major issues of that period: Sabbath observance and circumcision. The compiler clearly regarded the message of the stories as relevant to that period but did not alter them to make them fit it more closely. Perhaps this is an indication that the stories were already too well known for this to be acceptable. There has been some discussion in ch. 1 of the unity, or otherwise, of the authorship of the individual stories and of the role of the compiler in their use in the book.

Excursus 4: Daniel 12:11–12

There has been much inconclusive debate about the significance of the numbers in v. 12. Many see them as attempts to update the figure of 1,150 days in Dan 8:14 (if that is what the verse means). In context this is the period between the desecration of the Temple and its reconsecration. In fact, the period was somewhat shorter than this at three years and eight days. However, it is assumed that the compiler understood this as a prediction of when 'the end' (however it was understood) would come. When it did not come as expected he issued revised predictions. There are three problems with this view. First, there is the practicality of the idea of rapidly producing and circulating copies of a hand-produced book (see Porteus, 1979: 172). Then there is the likelihood that a series of failed predictions would damage the reputation of the book, which makes it hard to understand why it rapidly gained the status it did (so Newsom, 2014: 368). Finally, it does not explain the choice of the numbers.

Some attempts have been made to relate the periods to those between various pairs of events during the Antiochene period (e.g. Goldingay, 2019: 551–2). However, the information as to exact dates is limited and there is much latitude for speculation. No consensus has emerged.

In the second century a number of different calendars were in use by Jewish groups. This led to heated debates, such as between the Essenes and the Temple hierarchy, because of the cultic implications. In Dan 12:7 it is said that the period of suffering will last 'a time, times and half a time' (cf. 7:25). This is usually taken to mean three and a half years. The numbers are then taken as ways of calculating this period according to different calendars, but there is no exact match (see Nelson, 2012: 315 for examples).

The numbers, as is often the case in apocalypses, may have a symbolic significance which was clear to the original readers but is not to us (for a suggestion, see Newsom, 2014: 368).

The authorship of the Book of Daniel

Most of the scholars who accept a second-century date for the final form of Daniel think that the author/compiler of the book belonged to the group who are referred to as 'the wise' in Dan 11:33–35; 12:3. This is a group of learned Jews who 'give understanding to many' (11:33) and 'lead many to righteousness' (12:3). Presumably this would include passing on the message of resistance contained in Daniel. Some have tried to identify 'the wise' with one of the resistance groups mentioned in 1 Macc. 1–2, usually the 'Hasideans/Hasidim' (2:42). We have mentioned this group in ch. 4. The problem with this is that the Hasidim were willing to join the Maccabees in armed resistance until Alcimus replaced Menelaus as High Priest. However, as we saw in ch.4, 'the wise' were advocates of non-violent public resistance to Antiochus IV. They seem to be a group who are not mentioned in any other source than Daniel.

Who, then, was 'Daniel' for whom the book is named? He could simply have been the exilic Judean depicted in the stories. However, because of the affinity of Daniel with Jewish apocalypses, many scholars argue that the book is pseudonymous since that is the case with all the apocalypses, except *Revelation* in the New Testament. They are attributed to prominent figures from the past, such as Adam, Enoch and Moses. In fact, pseudonymity is found in many genres of that period and there is debate about the reason for it. With regard to the apocalypses which contain surveys of history it is often argued that pseudonymity is a way of enhancing their authority by presenting this as a prophecy of events to come by an ancient figure in the distant past. Others point out that we know that the neo-Pythagoreans attributed their writings to Pythagoras as a mark of respect for him and his teachings. It is noted that Jewish pseudepigraphical books carry the name of figures appropriate to their content. Mead (1987:102) argues that 'in the apocalyptic tradition, attribution is primarily a claim to authoritative tradition, not a statement of literary origin.' A different view is taken by Rowland (1982: 243) who suggests that in the apocalypses, pseudonymity may have its roots in the visionary experience because of 'the occurrence, in visionary literature of diverse origins, of the tendency of the visionary to separate his normal experience and his visionary life by speaking of the latter as if it happened to another person.'

If the author(s) of Daniel were using a hero from the distant past to lend authority to the book, who was he? Some scholars have tried to link Daniel with a person who is mentioned alongside Noah and Job in their righteousness in Ezek 14:14, 20 and also mentioned in Ezek 28:3 as being wise. The association with Noah and Job implies that he lived in the distant past. English translations name this person as 'Daniel.' However, in the Hebrew text the name is spelt *dāniēl* not *dāniyēʾl* as in the book of Daniel and nothing else is known of him in the Hebrew Bible. There is a righteous king called Danʾel mentioned in Ugaritic texts (KTU 1.17; see Wyatt, 1998, 246–77), but it is simply speculation to suggest linking him with the figure in Ezekiel. So is making a link between that figure and Daniel in the book of Daniel (for a fuller discussion, see Nelson, 2012: 17–18). Probably all we can say is that the author(s) of the visions in Daniel put themselves in the same tradition of teaching as presented in the stories, but developed that tradition to respond to a new situation.

The provenance of the Book of Daniel

There is a general consensus among scholars, whether they date Daniel to the sixth or the second century, that the book originated in Judea. Two main reasons are given for this. The first is the concentration on Jerusalem and the

Temple in Dan 6–12, and the second is that what is said of 'the wise' in Dan 11:33–35 is taken to imply their presence and activity in Judea during the Antiochene persecution. As discussed above, the author/compiler of Daniel is widely held to have belonged to this group.

However, there are some problems with this position. There is a general consensus that the stories in Dan 1–6 originated in the eastern diaspora and are shaped to commend 'a lifestyle for diaspora.' These stories could, of course, have become known in Judea but it would be a bit surprising if a Palestinian Jew facing the Antiochene persecution chose to use these stories as a basis for a 'tract for the times' without modifying them to make them more directly relevant to the current situation in Judea so that the picture of the Gentile kings was less positive and issues such as circumcision and Sabbath observance were addressed. Also, in the discussion of the visions in ch. 3 it was argued that there is evidence of a Babylonian provenance in the creation imagery and imagery of the bizarre beasts in ch. 7 and in the unusual literary form of the surveys of history in Dan. 8:23–25; 11:3–45. It is possible, of course, that the author of the visions was a Jew who had returned to Judea after living in the diaspora in Babylon.

An alternative to the general consensus is the possibility that Daniel was written/compiled in the eastern diaspora (Lucas, 2000). Psalm 137 and Neh 1 show that Jews in the diaspora could have a passionate concern for Jerusalem and the Temple such as is indicated in Dan 1:1–2; 5:23; 9:3–19. Also, Jer 29 and Neh 1 show that communication took place between the Jews in Jerusalem and those in the diaspora. Some have questioned how long it would take for news of the persecution in Judea to reach Jews in Babylon. If, as implied in the stories in Daniel, some of the group from which the book came were senior officials in the imperial administration (Newsom, 2014, 336, thinks this is 'not implausible'), they could have received the news quite rapidly through official channels.

One factor in the assumption that the book originated in Judea is the widespread view that apocalyptic movements arise in groups that see themselves as oppressed and/or marginalized. Although 1 Macc 1:41–43 claims that Antiochus' policy which led to persecution in Judea was applied throughout the empire, there is no real evidence that this was the case and that Jews elsewhere were affected by it. There is, though, evidence of religious conflict and subsequent repression in Babylon at about the time of the persecution in Judea. This came about because of Antiochus' actions against the Temple of Marduk in Babylon (Eddy, 2020: 135–6). Jews in the city may have feared that they would get caught up in this repression. More important, however, is the evidence collected by Cook (1995) that millennial movements, including apocalyptic ones, have arisen from a wide spectrum of social situations. They may arise from groups in positions of power and dominance as well as those dominated by others and powerless to do anything to change their situation. He argues that more important in explaining why a group becomes millennial than their social situation is their original world view. An especially important factor is a linear view of history and belief in a god outside history. Another important factor is the appearance of a catalyst which brings out the millennialism latent in the group's world view. This may be a teacher, a visionary or a written work. Although Cook does not mention it explicitly, his examples show that the catalyst may also be a change in the group's social situation. The group behind Dan 1–6 were heirs to the Hebrew prophets' view that history follows a linear course with the God of Israel as the sovereign over history. This view is expressed in the dream in Dan 2, but the theology of this chapter is not an apocalyptic one. The catalyst that transformed the world view of the group that preserved the stories seems to have been the change in the social situation, the Antiochene persecution of faithful Jews. This challenged the central assumption of the stories that serving a Gentile ruler, with the aim of bringing praise to the God of Israel, was possible for faithful Jews. The 'cognitive dissonance' this produced, even though the Jews in Babylon were not experiencing persecution themselves, prompted the apocalyptic re-interpretation of their traditions. A visionary, or visionaries, played a role in this. Maybe, like Jeremiah, whose writings influenced this group (Dan 9:2), who sent a letter to the exiles in Babylonia, to encourage and guide them, this group sent some of their number ('the wise') to Judea to convey to the Jews there their teaching and encouragement to stand firm in non-violent opposition to Antiochus' persecution. They were prepared to risk martyrdom in doing this.

Investigation

Make your own summary of the evidence and arguments given in this Study Guide concerning the date, authorship and provenance of *Daniel*. Draw your own conclusions, giving the reasons for them.

Appendix: The additions to *Daniel*

The Greek text of Daniel survives in two forms: the Old Greek (OG) and Theodotion's translation. Both contain additional passages not found in the Hebrew Bible. Because these were included in the Latin Vulgate translation of the Old Testament, the Council of Trent (1546) accepted them as part of the Roman Catholic canon of the Old Testament. Earlier, in his German translation of the Old Testament (1534), Luther put these books, with some others found in the LXX and the Vulgate but not in the Hebrew Bible, between the Old Testament and New Testament with the title 'Apocrypha, that is books which are not held equal to the sacred Scriptures, and nevertheless are useful and good to read'. Other Protestants adopted this practice.

The Prayer of Azariah and the Song of the Three Young Men

This is inserted between Dan 3:23 and 3:24 of the Hebrew form of the book. There are three parts. The Prayer of Azariah is a communal confession of sin and plea for mercy, which does not really fit the context in Dan 3. There is debate about whether its original language was Greek, Hebrew or Aramaic. It is followed by a short prose passage which was probably added to smooth the rather abrupt transition in the MT from the throwing of the three young men into the furnace to the king's expression of astonishment. It presupposes what has gone before in the story and is generally held to have been composed in Greek. The third part, the Song of the Three Young Men, begins with a section of declarative praise which is followed by a section in which 'all the works of the Lord' are called upon to praise him. This section has found a place in Christian liturgy as the *Benedicite*. There is a general consensus that the Song was originally composed in Hebrew.

These additions are pious embellishments of the story which serve to give further glory to God and to underline the divine origin of the three young men's deliverance.

Bel and the Dragon (or Serpent)

These are two separate stories which together form ch. 13 in Theodotion's translation, but ch. 14 in the OG and Vulgate. Their original language is uncertain because of some Semitisms in the Greek text. The opening verses of the OG identify Daniel as a priest and 'son of Abal', indicating a lack of knowledge of the Hebrew book of Daniel. Inaccuracies in the portrayal of Babylonian religion are often seen as evidence that the stories originated in Judea, not Babylonia. They may, however, be deliberate distortions to enhance the polemic of the stories.

Although Daniel is a companion of the king in the stories these are not court tales like those in Dan 1–6. Daniel's enemies are not other courtiers but priests and the general populace. Daniel provokes the opposition by his attacks on the priests and the idols they worship. The message of the two stories is that idolatry is false and not to be tolerated. The stories end with Daniel being thrown into a lion's den and being kept safe miraculously. When discussing the compilation of Daniel in ch. 1, it was noted that this story differs considerably from the one in Dan 6 and there are no grounds for supposing any interdependence between the two accounts.

Susanna

The story of Susanna is ch. 13 in the OG and Vulgate. In Theodotion's translation it precedes ch. 1. This is probably because it presents Daniel as an unknown young man, not a courtier. Some think Greek is the original language of the story because of a couple of striking puns in it. Others point to Semitisms and other oddities in the Greek as evidence of a Hebrew original, with the Greek puns being introduced by the translator.

The story is not a court tale. Daniel's opponents are fellow Jews, not pagans. It has similarities to the Greek romances. The central issue is not

Jewish identity but personal morality. In it, Daniel uses skilful questioning to prove that Susanna, a beautiful young widow, has been wrongly accused of adultery by her accusers, who are put to death as false witnesses. The main point of the story is Susanna's resolve to die rather than commit adultery, and her trust in God's knowledge of her innocence.

Bibliography

Commentaries

Montgomery's comprehensive commentary provides a valuable summary of the scholarly debates about Daniel up to when the commentary was written. There is still value in his detailed discussion of the Hebrew and Aramaic text of Daniel. Collins also provides a comprehensive commentary, taking a literary approach based on form-critical analysis. The long and informative introduction includes an essay by A. Y. Collins on 'The influence of Daniel on the New Testament.' Goldingay's commentary is an updated and expanded version of his earlier (1989) commentary. He takes a literary and theological approach and interacts with the newer trends in the study of Daniel since the 1990s, evidencing a wide knowledge of the secondary literature. Smith-Christopher was one of the early scholars to apply a post-colonial reading approach to Daniel. As well as providing a literary and theological study of Daniel, Lucas (2002) applies insights from ancient Near Eastern history, literature and religion to an understanding the book. There is also some discussion of inter-textuality. The ancient Near Eastern background is dealt with in more detail in Lucas (2009). Newsom's commentary is a replacement of the earlier one by Porteus in the same series. She takes a literary approach and seeks to understand the book in its historical and social context. Her interest in the book's ideology of sovereignty is developed in dialogue with post-colonial readings. The commentary also has very informative sections on the history of reception of Daniel at the end of the study of each chapter. These are written by B. W. Breed. House's commentary replaces Baldwin's commentary in the same series. These take a conservative approach to the authorship and date of Daniel.

Baldwin, J. G. (1978), *Daniel*, TOTC, Leicester: IVP.
Collins, J. J. (1993), *Daniel*, Hermeneia, Minneapolis, MN: Fortress.
Collins, J. J. (1998), *The Apocalyptic Imagination*, 2nd ed., Grand Rapids, MI: Eerdmans.
Driver, S. R. (1900), *The Book of Daniel*, CBC, Cambridge: Cambridge University Press.
Goldingay, J. (2019), *Daniel*, rev. ed., WBC, Grand Rapids, MI: Zondervan.

Hartman, L. F. and A. A. Di Lella (1978), *The Book of Daniel*, AB, Garden City, NY: Doubleday.

Heaton, E. (1956), *Daniel*, TBC, London: SCM.

House, P. R. (2018), *Daniel*, TOTC, London: IVP.

Lacocque, A. (1979), *The Book of Daniel*, London: SPCK.

Lucas, E. C. (2002), *Daniel*, ApOTC, Leicester: IVP.

Lucas, E. C. (2009), 'Daniel', in *Zondervan Illustrated Bible Backgrounds Commentary*, Vol. 4, 518–75. Edited by J. Walton, Grand Rapids, MI: Zondervan.

Montgomery, J. A. (1927), *The Book of Daniel*, ICC, Edinburgh: T. & T. Clark.

Nelson, W. B. (2012), *Daniel*, Grand Rapids, MI: Baker Books.

Newsom, C. A. with B. W. Breed (2014), *Daniel*, OTL, Louisville, KY: Westminster John Knox.

Pace, S. (2008), *Daniel*, Macon, GA: Smyth & Helwys.

Porteus, N. (1979), *Daniel*, rev. ed., OTL, London: SCM.

Smith-Christopher, D. L. (1996), 'Daniel', in *The New Interpreter's Bible*, Vol. 7, 19–152. Edited by L. E. Keck et al., Nashville, TN: Abingdon.

Young, E. J. (1972), *Daniel*, Geneva Commentaries, Edinburgh: Banner of Truth.

Other sources

Baker, D. W. (1980), 'Further Examples of the *Waw Explicativum*', *VT* 30: 129–36.

Beasley-Murray, G. R. (1983), 'The Interpretation of Daniel 7', *CBQ* 45: 44–58.

Beaulieu, P.-A. (1989), *The Reign of Nabonidus King of Babylon 556–539 B.C.*, New Haven, CT: Yale University Press.

Boyce, M. (1975, 1982), *A History of Zoroastrianism*, 2 vols, HO, Leiden: Brill.

Brenner, A. (2001), 'Who's Afraid of Feminist Criticism? Who's Afraid of Biblical Humour? The Case of the Obtuse Foreign Ruler in the Hebrew Bible', in *Prophets and Daniel: A Feminist Companion to the Bible (Second Series)*, 228–44. Edited by Athalya Brenner, London: Sheffield Academic Press.

Carley, K. W. (1975), *Ezekiel among the Prophets*, SBT (2nd Series) 31, London: SCM.

Colless, B. E. (1982), 'Cyrus the Persian as Darius the Mede in the Book of Daniel', *JSOT* 56: 113–26.

Collins, J. J. (1974), *The Sibylline Oracles of Egyptian Judaism*, SBLDS, Missoula, MO: Scholars Press.

Collins, J. J. (1979), *Apocalypse: The Morphology of a Genre*, Semeia 14, Missoula, MO: Scholars.

Colpe, C. (1961), *Die religionsgeschichtliche Schule*, FRLANT 78, Göttingen: Vandenhoeck & Rupecht.

Cook, S. L. (1995), *Prophecy and Apocalypticism*, Minneapolis, MN: Fortress.

Coxon, P. W. (1973), 'Greek Loan-Words and Alleged Greek Loan Translations in the Book of Daniel', *TGUOS* 25: 24–40.

Coxon, P. W. (1976), 'Daniel III 17: A Linguistic and Theological Problem', *VT* 26: 400–9.

Day, J. (1985), *God's Conflict with the Dragon and the Sea*, Cambridge: Cambridge University Press.

Eddy, S. K. (2020), *The King is Dead*, Eugene, OR: Wipf & Stock. This is a facsimile reprint of the original 1961 edition.

Emerton, J. A. (1958), 'The Origin of the Son of Man Imagery', *JTS* 9: 225–42.

Fewell, D. N. (1991), *Circle of Sovereignty: Plotting Politics in the Book of Daniel*, Nashville, TN: Abingdon.

Fishbane, M. (1988), *Biblical Interpretation in Ancient Israel*, Oxford: Clarendon.

Gadd, C. J. (1929), *History and Monuments of Ur*, London: Chatto & Windus.

Grabbe, L. L. (1979), 'Chronography in Jewish Hellenistic Historiography', *SBLSP* 17: 43–68.

Grabbe, L. L., (1988), 'Another Look at the *Gestalt* of "Darius the Mede"', *CBQ* 50: 198–213.

Grayson, A. K. (1975), *Assyrian and Babylonian Chronicles*, TCS, Locust Valley, NY: Augustin.

Grayson, A. K. and W. G. Lambert (1964), 'Akkadian Prophecies', *JCS* 18: 7–30.

Gunkel, H. (1895/2006), *Creation and Chaos in the Primeval Era and Eschaton*, Grand Rapids, MI: Eerdmans. This is a translation of the original 1895 German edition.

Hanson, P. D. (1976), 'Apocalypticism', *IDBSup*, 28–34.

Hasel, G. F. (1981), 'The Book of Daniel: Evidences Relating to Persons and Chronology', *AUSS* 19: 37–49.

Hellholm, D, (1986), 'The Problem of Apocalyptic Genre and the Apocalypse of John', *Semeia* 26: 13–64, Decatur, GA: Scholars.

Humphreys, W. L. (1973), 'A Life-Style for Diaspora: A Study of the Tales of Esther and Daniel', *JBL* 92: 211–23.

Koch, K. (1972), *The Rediscovery of Apocalyptic*, London: SCM.

Koch, K. (1986), *Daniel (1, 1–21)*, BKAT 22/1, Neukirchen-Vluyn: Neukirchener Verlag.

Konkel, A. H. (1997), 'Week', *NIDOTTE* 4: 20–4.

Laato, A. (1990), 'The Seventy Yearweeks in the Book of Daniel', *ZAW* 102: 212–25.

Lambert, W. G. (1978), *The Background of Jewish Apocalyptic*, London: Athlone.

Lucas, E. C. (2000), 'Daniel: Resolving the Enigma', *VT* 50: 66–80.

Mead, D. G. (1987), *Pseudonymity and Canon*, Grand Rapids, MI: Eerdmans.

Millard, A. R. (1977), 'Daniel 1–6 and History', *EvQ* 49: 67–73.

Millard, A. R. and P. Bordreuil (1982), 'A Statue from Syria with Assyrian and Aramaic Inscriptions', *BA* 45: 135–41.

Mosca, P. (1986), 'Ugarit and Daniel 7: A Missing Link', *Biblica* 67: 496–517.

Mowinckel, S. (1956), *He that Cometh*, Oxford: Basil Blackwell.

Müller, H.-P. (1972), 'Mantische Weisheit und Apokalyptic', *SVT* 22: 268–93.

Niditch, S. (1983), *The Symbolic Vision in Biblical Tradition*, HSM 30, Chico, CA: Scholars.

Nissinen, M (ed.) (2000), *Prophecy in Its Ancient Near Eastern Context: Mesopotamian, Biblical, and Arabian Perspectives*, Atlanta, GA: SBL.

Oppenheim, A. L. (1956), 'The Interpretation of Dreams in the Ancient Near East', *TAPS* 46: 179–373.

Oppenheim, A. L. (1977), *Ancient Mesopotamia*, rev. ed., Chicago, IL: University of Chicago Press.

Porter, P. A. (1983), *Metaphors and Monsters*, ConBOT 20, Malmö: Gleerup.

Portier-Young, A. (2011), *Apocalypse against Empire: Theologies of Resistance in Early Judaism*, Grand Rapids: Eerdmans.

Rad, G. von (1965), *Old Testament Theology 2*, Edinburgh: Oliver & Boyd.

Redford, D. B. (1970), *A Study of the Biblical Story of Joseph*, VTSup 20, Leiden: Brill.

Rowland, C. (1982), *The Open Heaven: A Study of Apocalyptic in Judaism and Early Christianity*, New York: Crossroad.

Rowley, H. H. (1935), *Darius the Mede and the Four World Empires in the Book of Daniel*, Cardiff: University of Wales Press.

Vanderkam, J. C. (1992), 'Ahikar/Ahiqar (Person)', *ABD* 1: 113–15.

Wills, L. M. (1990), *The Jew in the Court of the Foreign King*, HDR 26, Minneapolis, MN: Fortress.

Wiseman, D. J. (1965), 'Some Historical Problems in the Book of Daniel', in *Notes on Some Problems in the Book of Daniel*, 9–18. Edited by D. J. Wiseman, T. C. Mitchell, R. Joyce, W. J. Martin and K. A. Kitchen. London: Tyndale.

Wiseman, D. J. (1985), *Nebuchadrezzar and Babylon*, Schweich Lectures 1983, Oxford: Oxford University Press.

Wyatt, N. (1998), *Religious Texts From Ugarit*, Sheffield: Sheffield Academic Press.

Index of ancient sources

Index of modern authors

Index of subjects